Early Praise for *Async JavaScript*

Async JavaScript is the first full book I've seen dedicated to a key topic in Java-Script development today: how to deal with concurrency and concurrent tasks without going crazy! For the sake of your sanity, check this out.

➤ Peter Cooper, editor of JavaScript Weekly

Trevor delivers a concise guide to writing asynchronous JavaScript with a perfect balance of browser and server-side examples. Part guide, part overview, wholly engaging, this book is a must-read for any JavaScript developer looking to level up.

➤ Wynn Netherland, co-host of The Changelog

This is a complete guide to the asynchronous realm of JavaScript. The concepts and tools covered by this book are essential to anyone willing to build full-blown, well-structured and efficient JavaScript applications.

➤ Julien Biezemans, Ruby/JavaScript developer, author of Cucumber.js

Async JavaScript

Build More Responsive Apps with Less Code

Trevor Burnham

The Pragmatic Bookshelf

Dallas, Texas • Raleigh, North Carolina

Pragmatic Bookshelf

Many of the designations used by manufacturers and sellers to distinguish their products are claimed as trademarks. Where those designations appear in this book, and The Pragmatic Programmers, LLC was aware of a trademark claim, the designations have been printed in initial capital letters or in all capitals. The Pragmatic Starter Kit, The Pragmatic Programmer, Pragmatic Programming, Pragmatic Bookshelf, PragProg and the linking *g* device are trademarks of The Pragmatic Programmers, LLC.

Every precaution was taken in the preparation of this book. However, the publisher assumes no responsibility for errors or omissions, or for damages that may result from the use of information (including program listings) contained herein.

Our Pragmatic courses, workshops, and other products can help you and your team create better software and have more fun. For more information, as well as the latest Pragmatic titles, please visit us at *http://pragprog.com*.

The team that produced this book includes:

Jacquelyn Carter (editor)
Kim Wimpsett (copyeditor)
David J Kelly (typesetter)
Janet Furlow (producer)
Juliet Benda (rights)
Ellie Callahan (support)

Printed in the United States of America.
ISBN-13: 978-1-937785-27-7
Printed on acid-free paper.
Book version: P1.0—November 2012

*Dedicated to Steve Jobs and to the generation
of entrepreneurs he inspired.*

Contents

Acknowledgments   ix

Introduction   xi

1. **Understanding JavaScript Events** 1
   1.1   Scheduling Events   1
   1.2   Types of Async Functions   4
   1.3   Writing Async Functions   7
   1.4   Handling Async Errors   12
   1.5   Un-nesting Callbacks   17
   1.6   What We've Learned   18

2. **Distributing Events** 19
   2.1   PubSub   20
   2.2   Evented Models   24
   2.3   Custom jQuery Events   26
   2.4   What We've Learned   28

3. **Promises and Deferreds** 31
   3.1   A Very Brief History of Promises   32
   3.2   Making Promises   33
   3.3   Passing Data to Callbacks   37
   3.4   Progress Notifications   38
   3.5   Combining Promises   39
   3.6   Binding to the Future with pipe   41
   3.7   jQuery vs. Promises/A   43
   3.8   Replacing Callbacks with Promises   44
   3.9   What We've Learned   45

4. **Flow Control with Async.js** 47
   4.1   The Async Ordering Problem   48
   4.2   Async Collection Methods   49

	4.3	Organizing Tasks with Async.js	53
	4.4	Dynamic Async Queuing	54
	4.5	Minimalist Flow Control with Step	58
	4.6	What We've Learned	59
5.	**Multithreading with Workers**	. . . .	**61**
	5.1	Web Workers	62
	5.2	Node Workers with cluster	64
	5.3	What We've Learned	67
6.	**Async Script Loading**	. . . .	**69**
	6.1	Limitations and Caveats	70
	6.2	Reintroducing the <script> Tag	70
	6.3	Programmatic Loading	74
	6.4	What We've Learned	79
A1.	**Tools for Taming JavaScript**	. . . .	**81**
	A1.1	TameJS	81
	A1.2	StratifiedJS	81
	A1.3	Kaffeine	82
	A1.4	Streamline.js	82
	A1.5	Node-Fibers	83
	A1.6	The Future of JavaScript: Generators	83

Acknowledgments

It was not love at first sight with me and JavaScript. Yet today, it's one of my two favorite programming languages. The other? Its little brother, CoffeeScript. The story of how I learned to stop worrying and love JavaScripting is a story shared by tens of thousands of programmers. I'd like to thank those who took JavaScript seriously from the start, shaping the rich development ecosystem the language enjoys today: John Resig, for creating the browser's *de facto* standard library, jQuery; Jeremy Ashkenas, for producing CoffeeScript and the rich yet minimalistic Backbone.js framework; Ryan Dahl, for giving the language a robust server environment; and all the other programmers who've proven through their work that JavaScript is a first-class language after all.

Of course, love alone didn't write this book. I'd like to thank the Pragmatic Bookshelf team for helping me thoroughly renovate my original KickStarted manuscript and raise it to the standard of quality that PragProg is famous for. Particular thanks go to managing editor Susannah Pfalzer, head honchos Dave Thomas and Andy Hunt, and most of all my editor, Jackie Carter. Their savvy and motivation have been invaluable.

Thanks also to my technical reviewers for this edition: Julien Biezemans, Christophe Porteneuve, Michael Ficarra, Travis Swicegood, and Lon Ingram. Special thanks to Karl Stolley for going above and beyond in multiple reviews. I'd also like to thank Stan Angeloff and Roly Fentanes for reviewing the original manuscript. Any remaining errors are entirely my fault.

Thanks, finally, to my employer, HubSpot, for supporting me as I brought this book to completion. After years of nomadic freelancing, I've finally found a home.

Trevor Burnham
trevorburnham@gmail.com
November 2012

Introduction

Originally devised to enhance web pages in Netscape 2.0, JavaScript is now faced with being a single-threaded language in a multimedia, multitasking, multicore world. Yet JavaScript has not only persevered since 1995, it's thrived. One after the other, potential rivals in the browser—Flash, Silverlight, and Java applets, to name a few—have come and (more or less) gone.

Meanwhile, when a programmer named Ryan Dahl wanted to build a new framework for event-driven servers, he searched the far reaches of computer science for a language that was both dynamic and single-threaded before realizing that the answer was right in front of him. And so, Node.js was born, and JavaScript became a force to be reckoned with in the server world.

How did this happen? As recently as 2001, Paul Graham wrote the following in his essay "The Other Road Ahead":[1]

> I would not even use JavaScript, if I were you... Most of the JavaScript I see on the Web isn't necessary, and much of it breaks.

Today, Graham is the lead partner at Y Combinator, the investment group behind Dropbox, Heroku, and hundreds of other start-ups—nearly all of which use JavaScript. As he put it in a revised version of the essay, "JavaScript now works."

When did JavaScript become a respectable language? Some say the turning point was Gmail (2004), which showed the world that with a heavy dose of Ajax you could run a first-class email client in the browser. Others say that it was jQuery (2006), which abstracted the rival browser APIs of the time to create a *de facto* standard. (As of 2011, 48 percent of the top 17,000 websites use jQuery.[2])

---

1. A revised version of this essay can be found at http://paulgraham.com/road.html. The original footnote can be found in the book *Hackers & Painters*.
2. http://appendto.com/jquery-overtakes-flash

Whatever the reason, JavaScript is here to stay. Apple got behind JavaScript with WebKit and Safari. Microsoft is getting behind JavaScript with Metro. Even Adobe is getting behind JavaScript with tools to generate HTML5 instead of Flash. What began as a humble browser feature has become arguably the most important programming language in the world.

Thanks to the ubiquity of web browsers, JavaScript has come closer than any other language to fulfilling Java's old promise of "write once, run anywhere." In 2007, Jeff Atwood coined *Atwood's law:*

> Any application that can be written in JavaScript will eventually be written in JavaScript.[3]

Trouble in Paradise

JavaScript was conceived to be a single-threaded language where asynchronous tasks are handled with events. When there are only a few potential events, event-based code is much simpler than multithreaded code. It's conceptually elegant, and it eliminates the need to wrap up data in mutexes and semaphores to make it thread-safe. But when a number of events are expected, with state that needs to be carried from one event to the next, that simplicity often gives way to a code structure so terrifying that it's been dubbed the *Pyramid of Doom.*

```
step1(function(result1) {
  step2(function(result2) {
    step3(function(result3) {
      // and so on...
    });
  });
});
```

"I love async, but I can't code like this," one developer famously complained on the Node.js Google Group.[4] But the problem isn't with the language itself; it's with the way programmers use the language. Dealing with complex sets of events in an elegant way is still frontier territory in JavaScript.

So, let's push the frontier forward! Let's prove to the world that even the most complex problems can be tackled with clean, maintainable JavaScript code.

---

3.   http://www.codinghorror.com/blog/2007/07/the-principle-of-least-power.html
4.   https://groups.google.com/forum/#!topic/nodejs/wzSUdkPlCWg

Who Is This Book For?

This book is aimed at intermediate JavaScripters. You should know how variables are scoped. Keywords like typeof, arguments, and this shouldn't faze you. Perhaps most importantly, you should understand that

```
func(function(arg) { return next(arg); });
```

is just a needlessly verbose way of writing

```
func(next);
```

except in rare cases. (See Reg Braithwaite's excellent article "Captain Obvious on JavaScript" for more examples of small but important functional idioms.)[5]

What you *don't* need to know is how asynchronous events are scheduled in JavaScript. We'll cover that in the next chapter.

Resources for Learning JavaScript

As JavaScript has become the *lingua franca* of the Web (not to mention mobile devices), a vast number of informative books, courses, and sites devoted to it have appeared. Here are a few that I recommend:

- If you're new to programming altogether, check out the interactive tutorial site Codecademy.[6]

- If you're coming from another language and want to get up and running with JavaScript as a language for scripting the browser, take the interactive jQuery Air courses on CodeSchool.[7]

- If you want a more formal introduction to the JavaScript language, absorb Marijn Haverbeke's *Eloquent JavaScript*.[8]

- If you're a JavaScript beginner who wants to level up and avoid common pitfalls, spend some time in the JavaScript Garden.[9]

Where to Turn for Help?

When pondering questions like "Should I use typeof or instanceof here?" steer clear of the dated W3Schools site (which, regrettably, tends to be favored by Google searches). Instead, head to the Mozilla Developer Network (MDN).[10]

---

5. https://github.com/raganwald/homoiconic/blob/master/2012/01/captain-obvious-on-javascript.md
6. http://www.codecademy.com/
7. http://www.codeschool.com/
8. http://eloquentjavascript.net/
9. http://javascriptgarden.info/
10. https://developer.mozilla.org/

The Mozilla Foundation (you may have heard of its browser, Firefox) is headed up by Brendan Eich, the creator of JavaScript. The foundation knows its stuff.

If you can't find your answer among MDN's pages, take your question to Stack Overflow.[11] The site has fostered an amazingly helpful developer community, and it's a safe bet that any coherent question tagged JavaScript will receive a punctual response.

Running the Code Examples

This book is a bit unusual, in that I discuss both client-side (browser) and server-side (Node.js) code. That reflects the uniquely portable nature of JavaScript. The central concepts apply to all JavaScript environments, but certain examples are aimed at one or the other.

Even if you have no interest in writing Node applications, I hope you'll follow along by running these code snippets locally. See *Running Code in Node.js*, on page xiv for directions.

Which Examples Are Runnable?

When you see a code snippet with a filename, that means it's self-contained and can be run without modification. Here's an example:

Preface/stringConstructor.js
```
console.log('str'.constructor.name);
```

The surrounding context should make it clear whether the code is runnable in the browser, in Node.js, or in both.

When a code snippet doesn't have a filename, that means it's not self-contained. It may be part of a larger example, or it may be a hypothetical. Here's an example:

```
var tenSeconds = 10 * 1e3;
setTimeout(launchSatellite, tenSeconds);
```

These examples are meant to be read, not run.

Running Code in Node.js

Node is very easy to install and use: just head to http://nodejs.org/, click Download, and run the Windows or OS X installer (or build from source on *nix). You can then run node from the command line to open a JavaScript REPL (analogous to Ruby's irb environment).

---

11. http://stackoverflow.com/

```
$ node
> Math.pow(5, 6)
15625
```

You can run a JavaScript file by giving its name as an argument to the node command.

```
$ echo "console.log(typeof NaN)" > foo.js
$ node foo.js
number
```

Running Code in the Browser

Every modern browser provides a nice little REPL that lets you run JavaScript code in the context of the current page. But for playing with multiline code examples, you're better off using a web sandbox like jsFiddle.[12]

With jsFiddle, you can enter JavaScript, HTML, and CSS, and then click Run (or press Ctrl+Enter) to see the result. (console output will go to your developer console.) You can bring in a framework like jQuery by choosing it in the left sidebar. And you can save your work, giving you a shareable URL.

Code Style in This Book

JavaScript has no official style guide, but maintaining a consistent style within a project is important. For this book, I've adopted the following (very common) conventions:

- Two-space indentation
- camelCase identifiers
- Semicolons at the end of every expression, except function definitions

More esoterically, I've adopted a special convention for indentation in a chain of function calls, based on a proposal by Reg Braithwaite. The rule is, essentially, that two function calls in a chain have the same indentation level if and only if they return the same object. So, for instance, I might write the following:

```
$('#container > ul li.inactive')
.slideUp();
```

jQuery's slideUp method returns the same object that it was called on. Thus, it isn't indented. By contrast:

```
var $paragraphClone = $('p:last')
  .clone();
```

---

12. http://jsfiddle.net/

Here, the clone method is indented because it returns a different object.

The advantage of this convention is that it clarifies what each function in a chain is returning. Here's a more complex example:

```
$('h1')
  .first()
  .addClass('first')
.end()
  .last()
  .addClass('last');
```

jQuery's first and last filter a set down to its first and last elements, while end undoes the last filter. So, end is unindented because it returns the same value as $('h1'). (last is allowed to occupy the same indentation level as first because the chain was reset.)

This approach to indentation is especially useful when we're doing functional programming, as we'll see in Chapter 4, *Flow Control with Async.js*, on page 47.

```
[1, 2, 3, 4, 5]
  .filter(function(int) { return int % 2 === 1; })
    .forEach(function(odd) { console.log(odd); })
```

A Word on altJS

A number of languages compile to JavaScript, making code easier to write. (You can find a fairly comprehensive list at http://altjs.org.) This book isn't about them. It's about writing the best JavaScript code we can without the use of a precompiler. I have nothing against altJS (see the next section), but I believe it's important to understand the underlying language.

Some altJS languages are aimed specifically at "taming" async callbacks by allowing them to be written in a more synchronous style. I've included an overview of these languages in Appendix 1, *Tools for Taming JavaScript*, on page 81.

CoffeeScript

It's no secret that I ♥ CoffeeScript, a beautiful and expressive language that compiles to JavaScript. I use it extensively in my day-to-day work at HubSpot. I've given talks on it at conferences like Railsconf and Øredev. And it was the subject of my first book, *CoffeeScript: Accelerated JavaScript Development.*[13]

---

13. http://pragprog.com/book/tbcoffee/coffeescript

But when I started writing the book you're reading now, I decided that doing it in CoffeeScript would needlessly limit its appeal. By and large, Coffee-Scripters understand JavaScript perfectly well, whereas code like square = (x) => x * x might as well be hieroglyphics to JavaScript purists.[14]

So, if you're a CoffeeScripter, my apologies for the curly braces. Rest assured that the lessons you draw from this book will carry over to any altJS language.

Resources for This Book

This book has a website at http://pragprog.com/book/tbajs/async-javascript. There you can download the example code used in the book, get up-to-date information, and ask book-related questions in a friendly forum.

For more general JavaScript-related questions, I (again) heartily recommend Stack Overflow.[15] I have no affiliation with the site, but I am an avid fan with a proud 23,000 reputation points (and counting). Coherent, well-formatted questions there are almost always answered promptly.

Finally, if you want to contact me directly, you can reach me at trevorburnham@gmail.com or on Twitter: @trevorburnham. I'm always happy to hear from my readers.

Enough introduction. Let's get our async on!

---

14. However, maybe not for long: http://wiki.ecmascript.org/doku.php?id=harmony:arrow_function_syntax.
15. http://stackoverflow.com/

CHAPTER 1

Understanding JavaScript Events

Events. How *do* they work? Confusion about JavaScript's asynchronous event model is as old as JavaScript itself. Confusion leads to bugs, bugs lead to anger, and Yoda taught us the rest....

Yet at heart, JavaScript events are both conceptually elegant and practical. Once you've accepted the language's single-threaded design, it feels like a feature rather than a limitation. It means that your code is uninterruptible and that the events you schedule line up in an orderly fashion.

In this chapter, we'll take a tour of JavaScript's asynchronous mechanisms and dispel some common misconceptions. We'll see what setTimeout *really* does. Then we'll discuss handling errors in callbacks. Finally, we'll set up the main theme of this book: organizing async code for clarity and maintainability.

1.1 Scheduling Events

When we want to make a piece of code run in the future in JavaScript, we put it in a *callback*. A callback is just an ordinary function, except that it's passed to a function like setTimeout or bound as a property like document.onready. When a callback runs, we say that an event (e.g., the timeout elapsing or the document becoming ready) has fired.

Of course, the devil is in the details, even for something as seemingly simple as setTimeout. A common description of setTimeout goes something like this:

> Given a callback and a delay of n milliseconds, setTimeout runs that callback n milliseconds later.

But as we'll see in this section, and throughout this chapter, that description is seriously flawed. In most cases, it's only approximately true. In others, it's flat-out wrong. To truly understand setTimeout, we have to understand the JavaScript event model as a whole.

Now or Later?

To begin our exploration of setTimeout, let's look at a simple example of a situation that often mystifies new JavaScripters, especially those coming from multithreaded languages like Java and Ruby.

```
EventModel/loopWithTimeout.js
for (var i = 1; i <= 3; i++) {
  setTimeout(function(){ console.log(i); }, 0);
};
```

❮ 4
4
4

Most newcomers to the language would expect the loop to produce the output 1, 2, 3, or perhaps a juxtaposition of those three numbers as the three timeouts (each scheduled to go off in 0 milliseconds) race to fire first.

To understand why the output is 4, 4, 4 instead, there are three things you need to know.

- There's only one variable named i, scoped by the declaration var i (which, incidentally, scopes it not within the loop but within the closest function containing the loop).

- After the loop, i === 4, having been incremented until it failed the condition i <= 3.

- JavaScript event handlers don't run until the thread is free.

The first two concepts are in the realm of JavaScript 101, but the third comes as more of a surprise. When I first started using JavaScript, I didn't quite believe it. Java had trained me to fear that my code could be interrupted *at any moment*. A million potential edge cases filled me with anxiety as I wondered, "What if a rare event happened between these two lines of code?"

And then one day, that burden was lifted from me....

Blocking the Thread

This piece of code demolished my preconceptions about JavaScript events:

```
EventModel/loopBlockingTimeout.js
var start = new Date;
setTimeout(function(){
  var end = new Date;
  console.log('Time elapsed:', end - start, 'ms');
}, 500);
while (new Date - start < 1000) {};
```

In my multithreaded mind-set, I'd expected only 500ms to go by before the timed function ran. But that would have required the loop, designed to last a full second, to be interrupted. Instead, if you run the code, you'll get something like this:

❮ Time elapsed: 1002ms

You'll probably get a slightly different number; setTimeout and setInterval are, alas, a lot less precise than you'd hope (see *Timing Functions*, on page 5). But it will definitely be at least 1000, because the setTimeout callback can't fire until the while loop has finished running.

So, if setTimeout isn't using another thread, then what is it doing?

Meet the Queue

When we call setTimeout, a timeout event is *queued*. Then execution continues: the line after the setTimeout call runs, and then the line after that, and so on, until there are no lines left. Only then does the JavaScript virtual machine ask, "What's on the queue?"

If there's at least one event on the queue that's eligible to "fire" (like a 500ms timeout that was set 1000ms ago), the VM will pick one and call its *handler* (e.g., the function we passed in to setTimeout). When the handler returns, we go back to the queue.

Input events work the same way: when a user clicks a DOM element with a click handler attached, a click event is queued. But the handler won't be executed until all currently running code has finished (and, potentially, until after other events have had their turn). That's why web pages that use Java-Script imprudently tend to become unresponsive.

You might sometimes hear the term *event loop* used to describe how the queue works. It's as if your code is being run from a loop that looks like this:

```
runYourScript();
while (atLeastOneEventIsQueued) {
  fireNextQueuedEvent();
};
```

One implication of this is that each event that fires will be at the root of the stack trace. We'll learn more about that in Section 1.4, *Handling Async Errors*, on page 12.

The ease of event scheduling in JavaScript is one of the language's most powerful features. Async functions like setTimeout make delayed execution simple, without spawning threads. JavaScript code can never be interrupted, because events can be *queued* only while code is running; they can't *fire* until it's done.

In the next section, we'll take a closer look at the building blocks of async JavaScript.

1.2   Types of Async Functions

Each JavaScript environment comes with its own set of async functions. Some, like setTimeout and setInterval, are ubiquitous. Others are unique to certain browsers or server-side frameworks. The async functions provided by the JavaScript environment generally fall into two categories: I/O and timing. These are the basic building blocks that you'll use to define complex async behaviors in your applications.

I/O Functions

Node.js wasn't created so that people could run JavaScript on the server. It was created because Ryan Dahl wanted an event-driven server framework built on a high-level language. JavaScript just happened to be the right language for the job. Why? Because the language is a perfect fit for *nonblocking I/O*.

In other languages, it's tempting to "block" your application (typically by running a loop) until an I/O request completes. In JavaScript, that approach isn't even possible. A loop like this will run forever:

```
var ajaxRequest = new XMLHttpRequest;
ajaxRequest.open('GET', url);
ajaxRequest.send(null);
while (ajaxRequest.readyState === XMLHttpRequest.UNSENT) {
  // readyState can't change until the loop returns
};
```

Instead, you need to attach a handler and return to the event queue.

```
var ajaxRequest = new XMLHttpRequest;
ajaxRequest.open('GET', url);
ajaxRequest.send(null);
ajaxRequest.onreadystatechange = function() {
  // ...
};
```

That's how it goes. Whether you're waiting for a keypress from the user or a batch of data from a remote server, you need to define a callback—unless your JavaScript environment gives you a synchronous I/O function that does the blocking for you.

In the browser, Ajax methods have an async option that can (but *should never, ever*) be set to false, bringing the entire browser pane to a halt until a response is received. In Node.js, synchronous API methods are clearly indicated with names like fs.readFileSync. These are convenient when writing short scripts but should be avoided when writing applications that need to handle multiple requests or operations in parallel. And these days, which applications don't?

Some I/O functions have both synchronous and async effects. For instance, when you manipulate the DOM in a modern browser, the changes are immediate from your script's perspective but aren't rendered until you return to the event queue. That prevents the DOM from being rendered in an inconsistent state. You can see a simple demonstration of this at http://jsfiddle.net/TrevorBurnham/SNBYV/.

Is console.log Async?

WebKit's console.log has surprised many a developer by behaving asynchronously. In Chrome or Safari, this code will log {foo: bar}:

```
EventModel/log.js
var obj = {};
console.log(obj);
obj.foo = 'bar';
```

How does this happen? Rather than taking a snapshot of the object immediately, WebKit's console.log stores a reference to the object and then takes a snapshot when the code returns to the event queue.

Node's console.log, on the other hand, is strictly synchronous, so the same code yields the output {}.

Adapting to nonblocking I/O is one of the biggest hurdles that newcomers to JavaScript face, but it's also one of the language's key strengths. It makes writing efficient, event-based code feel natural.

Timing Functions

We've seen how async functions are a natural fit for I/O operations, but sometimes we want asynchronicity for its own sake. That is, we want to make a function run at some point in the future, perhaps for an animation or a simulation. The well-known functions for time-based events are setTimeout and its repeating cousin, setInterval.

Unfortunately, these well-known timer functions have their flaws. As we saw in *Blocking the Thread*, on page 2, one of those flaws is insurmountable: no JavaScript timing function can cause code to run while other code is running in the same JavaScript process. But even with that limitation in mind, setTimeout and setInterval are alarmingly imprecise. Here's a demonstration:

```
EventModel/fireCount.js
var fireCount = 0;
var start = new Date;
var timer = setInterval(function() {
  if (new Date - start > 1000) {
    clearInterval(timer);
    console.log(fireCount);
    return;
  }
  fireCount++;
}, 0);
```

When we schedule an event with setInterval and a 0ms delay, it should run as often as possible, right? So, in a modern browser powered by a speedy Intel i7 processor, at what rate does the event fire?

About 200/sec. That's across Chrome, Safari, and Firefox. Under Node, the event fired at a rate of about 1000/sec. (Using setTimeout to schedule each iteration yields similar results.) By comparison, replacing setInterval with a simple while loop brings that rate to 4,000,000/sec in Chrome and 5,000,000/sec in Node!

What's going on? It turns out that setTimeout and setInterval are slow by design. In fact, the HTML spec (which all major browsers respect) mandates a *minimum* timeout/interval of 4ms![1]

So, what do you do when you need finer-grained timing? Some runtimes offer alternatives.

- In Node, process.nextTick lets you schedule an event to fire ASAP. On my system, process.nextTick events fire at a rate of over 100,000/sec.

- Modern browsers (including IE9+) have a requestAnimationFrame function, which serves a dual purpose: it allows JavaScript animations to run at 60+ frames/sec, and it conserves CPU cycles by preventing those animations from running in background tabs. In the latest Chrome, you can even get submillisecond precision.[2]

Though they're the bread and butter of async JavaScript, never forget that setTimeout and setInterval are imprecise tools. When you just want to produce a

---

1. http://www.whatwg.org/specs/web-apps/current-work/multipage/timers.html#dom-windowtimers-settimeout
2. http://updates.html5rocks.com/2012/05/requestAnimationFrame-API-now-with-sub-millisecond-precision

short delay in Node, use process.nextTick. In the browser, try to use a shim[3] that defers to requestAnimationFrame in browsers that support it and falls back on setTimeout in those that don't.

That concludes our brief overview of basic async functions in JavaScript. But how do we tell when a function is async anyway? In the next section, we'll ponder that question as we write our own async functions.

1.3 Writing Async Functions

Every async function in JavaScript is built on some other async function(s). It's async functions all the way down (to native code)!

The converse is also true: any function that uses an async function has to provide the result of that operation in an async way. As we learned from *Blocking the Thread*, on page 2, JavaScript doesn't provide a mechanism for preventing a function from returning until an async operation has finished. In fact, until the function returns, no async events will fire.

In this section, we'll look at some common patterns in async function design. We'll see that functions can be mercurial, deciding to be async only some of the time. But first, let's define exactly what an async function is.

When Is a Function Async?

The term *async function* is a bit of a misnomer: if you call a function, your program simply won't continue until that function returns. What JavaScripters mean when they call a function "async" is that it can cause another function (called a *callback* when it's passed as an argument to the function) to run later, from the event queue. So, an async function that takes a callback will never fail this test:

```
var functionHasReturned = false;
asyncFunction(function() {
  console.assert(functionHasReturned);
});
functionHasReturned = true;
```

Another term for async functions is *nonblocking*. The term emphasizes how speedy they are: a query made with an async MySQL driver may take an hour, but the function that sent the query will return in a matter of microseconds —a boon to web servers that need to quickly process a high volume of incoming requests.

---

3.   http://paulirish.com/2011/requestanimationframe-for-smart-animating/

Typically, functions that take a callback take it as their last argument. (Regrettably, the venerable setTimeout and setInterval are exceptions to this convention.) But some async functions take callbacks indirectly, by returning a Promise or using PubSub. We'll learn about those patterns later in the book.

Unfortunately, the only way to be sure whether a function is async or not is to inspect its source code. Some functions that are synchronous have an API that looks async, either because they might become async in the future or because callbacks provide a convenient way to return multiple arguments. When in doubt, don't depend on a function being async.

Sometimes-Async Functions

There are functions that are async sometimes but not at other times. For instance, jQuery's eponymous function (typically aliased as $) can be used to delay a function until the DOM has finished loading. But if the DOM has already finished loading, there's no delay; its callback fires immediately.

This unpredictable behavior can get you in a lot of trouble if you aren't careful. One mistake I've seen (and made myself) is assuming that $ will run a function after other scripts on the page have loaded.

```
// application.js
$(function() {
  utils.log('Ready');
});
```

```
// utils.js
window.utils = {
  log: function() {
    if (window.console) console.log.apply(console, arguments);
  }
};
```

```
<script src="application.js"></script>
<script src="util.js"></script>
```

This code works fine—unless the browser loads the page from the cache, making the DOM ready before the script runs. When that happens, the callback passed to $ runs before utils.log is set, causing an error. (We could avoid this situation by taking a more modern approach to client-side dependency management. See Chapter 6, *Async Script Loading*, on page 69.)

Let's look at another example.

Async Functions with Caching

A common variety of sometimes-async functions is async request functions that cache their results. For example, suppose we're writing a browser-based calculator that uses web workers to run calculations in a separate thread. (We'll learn about the Web Worker API in Chapter 5, *Multithreading with Workers*, on page 61.) Our main script might look like this:[4]

```
var calculationCache = {},
    calculationCallbacks = {},
    mathWorker = new Worker('calculator.js');

mathWorker.addEventListener('message', function(e) {
  var message = e.data;
  calculationCache[message.formula] = message.result;
  calculationCallbacks[message.formula](message.result);
});

function runCalculation(formula, callback) {
  if (formula in calculationCache) {
    return callback(calculationCache[formula]);
  };
  if (formula in calculationCallbacks) {
    return setTimeout(function() {
      runCalculation(formula, callback);
    }, 0);
  };
  mathWorker.postMessage(formula);
  calculationCallbacks[formula] = callback;
}
```

Here, the runCalculation function is synchronous when the result has already been cached but is asynchronous otherwise. There are three possible scenarios.

- The formula has already been computed, so the result is in the calculationCache. In this case, runCalculation is synchronous.

- The formula has been sent to the worker, but the result hasn't been received yet. In this case, runCalculation sets a timeout to call itself again; the process will repeat until the result is in calculationCache.

- The formula hasn't yet been sent to the worker. In this case, we'll invoke the callback from the worker's 'message' event listener.

---

4. You can see a working version of this example at http://webworkersandbox.com/
   5009efc12245588e410002cf.

Notice that in scenarios 2 and 3, we're waiting for a task to be completed in two different ways. I wrote the example this way to illustrate common approaches when we're waiting for something to change, like the value of the cached computation. Should we prefer one approach over the other? Let's look at that next.

Async Recursion vs. Callback Storage

In runCalculation, we waited for the worker to finish its job by either repeating the same function call from a timeout (*async recursion*) or simply storing a callback.

Which approach is best? At first glance, it might seem easiest to use only async recursion, eliminating the need for the calculationCallbacks object. Newcomers to JavaScript often use setTimeout for this purpose because it resembles a common idiom of thread-based languages. A Java version of this program would probably have a loop like this:

```
while (!calculationCache.get(formula)) {
  Thread.sleep(0);
};
```

But timeouts aren't free. In large numbers, they can create a significant computational load. The scary thing about async recursion is that there's no limit to the number of timeouts that could be firing while we wait for the job to finish. Plus, it makes our application's event structure unnecessarily complicated. For these reasons, async recursion should be regarded as an anti-pattern.

We can avoid async recursion in our calculator by storing an array of callbacks for each formula.

```
var calculationCache = {},
    calculationCallbacks = {},
    mathWorker = new Worker('calculator.js');
mathWorker.addEventListener('message', function(e) {
  var message = e.data;
  calculationCache[message.formula] = message.result;
  calculationCallbacks[message.formula]
  .forEach(function(callback) {
    callback(message.result);
  });
});

function runCalculation(formula, callback) {
  if (formula in calculationCache) {
    return callback(calculationCache[formula]);
  };
```

```
  if (formula in calculationCallbacks) {
    return calculationCallbacks[formula].push(callback);
  };
  mathWorker.postMessage(formula);
  calculationCallbacks[formula] = [callback];
}
```

Without the timeout, our code is much more straightforward, as well as more efficient.

In general, avoid async recursion. It's necessary only when you're dealing with a library that provides async functionality without any kind of callback mechanism. And if you're ever in that situation, the first thing you should do is write a patch for that library. Or find a better one.

Mixing Returns and Callbacks

In both of our implementations of runCalculation, we sometimes return a value. This was an arbitrary choice made for brevity. The line

```
return callback(calculationCache[formula]);
```

could easily have been written as

```
callback(calculationCache[formula]);
return;
```

because the return value isn't intended to be used. This is a common idiom in JavaScript, and it's usually harmless.

However, some functions both return a useful value and take a callback. In those cases, it's important to remember that the callback will be called either synchronously (before the return) or asynchronously (after the return).

Never define a potentially synchronous function that returns a value that might be useful in the callback. For example, this function that opens a WebSocket[5] connection to a given server (caching to ensure only one connection per server) violates that rule:

```
var webSocketCache = {};
function openWebSocket(serverAddress, callback) {
  var socket;

  if (serverAddress in webSocketCache) {
    socket = webSocketCache[serverAddress];

    if (socket.readyState === WebSocket.OPEN) {
      callback();
```

---

5. https://developer.mozilla.org/en/WebSockets/

```
    } else {
      socket.onopen = _.compose(callback, socket.onopen);
    };
  } else {
    socket = new WebSocket(serverAddress);
    webSocketCache[serverAddress] = socket;
    socket.onopen = callback;
  };
  return socket;
};
```

(This code relies on the Underscore.js library. _.compose defines a new function that runs both callback and the original socket.onopen callback.[6])

The problem with this code is that if the socket is already cached and open, then the callback will run before the function returns, breaking this code:

```
var socket = openWebSocket(url, function() {
  socket.send('Hello, server!');
});
```

The solution? Wrap the callback in a setTimeout.

```
if (socket.readyState === WebSocket.OPEN) {
  setTimeout(callback, 0);
} else {
  // ...
}
```

Using a timeout here may feel like a kludge, but it's much better than having an inconsistent API.

In this section, we've seen several best practices for writing async functions. Don't rely on a function always being async, unless you've read its source code. Avoid using timer methods to wait for something to change. When returning a value and running a callback from the same function, make sure the callback runs after the return.

This is a lot of information to take in at once, but writing good async functions is key to writing good JavaScript.

1.4 Handling Async Errors

Like many modern languages, JavaScript allows you to throw exceptions and catch them in a try/catch block. If uncaught, most environments will give you a helpful stack trace. For example, this code will throw an exception because '{' is invalid JSON:

---

6.   http://documentcloud.github.com/underscore/#compose

```
EventModel/stackTrace.js
function JSONToObject(jsonStr) {
  return JSON.parse(jsonStr);
}
var obj = JSONToObject('{');
```

❮ SyntaxError: Unexpected end of input
      at Object.parse (native)
      at JSONToObject (/AsyncJS/stackTrace.js:2:15)
      at Object.<anonymous> (/AsyncJS/stackTrace.js:4:11)

The stack trace tells us not only where the error was thrown from but also where the original mistake was made: line 4. Unfortunately, tracking down the causes of async errors isn't as straightforward. In this section, we'll see why throw is rarely the right tool for handling errors in callbacks and how async APIs are designed around this limitation.

Throwing from Callbacks

What happens when we throw an error from an async callback? Let's run a test.

```
EventModel/nestedErrors.js
setTimeout(function A() {
  setTimeout(function B() {
    setTimeout(function C() {
      throw new Error('Something terrible has happened!');
    }, 0);
  }, 0);
}, 0);
```

The result of this application is an extraordinarily short stack trace.

❮ Error: Something terrible has happened!
      at Timer.C (/AsyncJS/nestedErrors.js:4:13)

Wait a minute—what happened to A and B? Why aren't they in the stack trace? Well, because they weren't on the stack when C ran. Each of the three functions was run directly from the event queue.

For the same reason, we can't catch errors thrown from async callbacks with a try/catch block. Here's a demonstration:

```
EventModel/asyncTry.js
try {
  setTimeout(function() {
    throw new Error('Catch me if you can!');
  }, 0);
} catch (e) {
  console.error(e);
}
```

Do you see the problem here? Our try/catch block will catch only those errors that occur within the setTimeout function itself. Since setTimeout runs its callback asynchronously, even when the timeout is 0, the error it throws will go straight to our application's uncaught exception handler (see *Handling Uncaught Exceptions*, on page 14).

In general, putting a try/catch block around a function that takes an async callback is pointless. (The exception is when the async function does something synchronous and error-prone as well. Node's fs.watch(file, callback), for example, will throw an error if the target file doesn't exist.) That's why callbacks in Node.js almost always take an error as their first argument, allowing the callback to decide how to handle it. For example, this Node app tries to read a file asynchronously and logs any error (such as the file not existing):

```
EventModel/readFile.js
var fs = require('fs');
fs.readFile('fhgwgdz.txt', function(err, data) {
  if (err) {
    return console.error(err);
  };
  console.log(data.toString('utf8'));
});
```

Client-side JavaScript libraries are less consistent, but the most common pattern is for there to be separate callbacks for success and failure. jQuery's Ajax methods follow this pattern.

```
$.get('/data', {
  success: successHandler,
  failure: failureHandler
});
```

No matter what the API looks like, always remember that you can handle async errors only from within a callback. As an async Yoda might say, "Do, or do not. There is no try."

Handling Uncaught Exceptions

When we throw an exception from a callback, it's up to whomever calls the callback to catch it. But what if the exception is never caught? At that point, different JavaScript environments play by different rules....

In the Browser

Modern browsers show uncaught exceptions in the developer console and then return to the event queue. You can modify this behavior by attaching a handler to window.onerror. If the handler returns true, it'll prevent the browser's default error-handling behavior.

```
window.onerror = function(err) {
  return true;  // ignore all errors completely
};
```

In production, you might want to consider a JavaScript error-handling service, such as Errorception.[7] Errorception provides a ready-made window.onerror handler that reports all uncaught exceptions to their server, which can then send you notifications.

In Node.js

Node's analog to window.onerror is the process object's uncaughtException event. Normally, a Node app will exit immediately on an uncaught exception. But as long as at least one uncaughtException handler exists, the app will simply return to the event queue.

```
process.on('uncaughtException', function(err) {
  console.error(err); // shutdown averted!
});
```

However, as of Node 0.8.4, uncaughtException is deprecated. According to the docs,[8]

> uncaughtException is a very crude mechanism for exception handling and may be removed in the future...
>
> Don't use it, use domains instead.

What are domains? you ask. Domains are evented objects that convert throws into 'error' events. (We'll talk more about evented objects in Chapter 2, *Distributing Events*, on page 19.) Here's an example:

EventModel/domainThrow.js
```
var myDomain = require('domain').create();
myDomain.run(function() {
  setTimeout(function() {
    throw new Error('Listen to me!')
  }, 50);
});

myDomain.on('error', function(err) {
  console.log('Error ignored!');
});
```

---

7.   http://errorception.com/

8.   http://nodejs.org/docs/latest/api/process.html#process_event_uncaughtexception

The throw from the timeout event simply triggers the domain's error handler.

❮ Error ignored!

Magical, isn't it? Domains make throw much more palatable. Unfortunately, they're available only in Node 0.8+, and as of this writing, they're still considered an experimental feature. For more information, see the Node docs.[9]

Whether you're in the browser or on the server, global exception handlers should be seen as a measure of last resort. Use them only for debugging.

To Throw or Not to Throw?

When you're given an error, the easiest thing to do with it is to throw it. In Node code, you'll often see callbacks that look like this:

```
function(err) {
  if (err) throw err;
  // ...
}
```

We'll use this idiom frequently in Chapter 4, *Flow Control with Async.js*, on page 47. But in a production app, allowing routine exceptions and fatal errors alike to bubble up to the global handler is unacceptable. throw in a callback is a JavaScripter's way of saying, "I don't want to think about this right now."

What about throwing exceptions that you know will be caught? That's an equally thorny area. In 2011, Isaac Schlueter (creator of npm and current head of Node development) argued that try/catch is an anti-pattern.[10]

> Try/catch is goto wrapped in pretty braces. There's no way to continue where you left off, once the error is handled. What's worse, in the code that throws, you have no idea where you're jumping to. When you return an error code, you are fulfilling a contract. When you throw, you're saying, "I know I was talking to you, but I'm going to jump over you now and talk to your boss instead." It's rude. If it's not an emergency, don't do that; if it is an emergency, then we should crash.

Schlueter advocated using throws purely as assert-like constructs, a way of bringing applications to a halt when they're doing something completely unexpected. The Node community has largely followed this recommendation, though that may change with the emergence of domains.

So, what's the current best practice for handling async errors? I suggest heeding Schlueter's advice: if you want your whole application to stop, go ahead and use throw. Otherwise, give some thought as to how the error should

---

9. http://nodejs.org/docs/latest/api/domain.html
10. https://groups.google.com/forum/#!topic/nodejs/1ESsssIxrUU

be handled. Do you want to show the user an error message? Retry the request? Sing "Daisy Bell"? Then handle it like that, as close to the source as possible.

1.5 Un-nesting Callbacks

The most common anti-pattern in JavaScript is nesting callbacks within callbacks. Remember the Pyramid of Doom from the introduction? Let's look at a concrete example that you might see in a Node server.

```
function checkPassword(username, passwordGuess, callback) {
  var queryStr = 'SELECT * FROM user WHERE username = ?';
  db.query(selectUser, username, function (err, result) {
    if (err) throw err;
    hash(passwordGuess, function(passwordGuessHash) {
      callback(passwordGuessHash === result['password_hash']);
    });
  });
}
```

Here we've defined an async function (checkPassword), which fires another async function (db.query), which potentially fires another async function (hash). (It's impossible to know for certain whether these functions are async without actually reading their code, but it's reasonable to assume so here.)

What's the problem with this code? Right now, nothing. It works, and it's succinct. But it's going to get awfully hairy when we try to add new features to it, like handling that database error instead of throwing it (see *To Throw or Not to Throw?*, on page 16), logging access attempts, throttling, and so on.

Nested callbacks tempt us to add more features by adding more code, rather than implementing those features in manageable, reusable pieces. This equivalent implementation of checkPassword avoids that temptation:

```
function checkPassword(username, passwordGuess, callback) {
  var passwordHash;
  var queryStr = 'SELECT * FROM user WHERE username = ?';
  db.query(selectUser, username, queryCallback);

  function queryCallback(err, result) {
    if (err) throw err;
    passwordHash = result['password_hash'];
    hash(passwordGuess, hashCallback);
  }

  function hashCallback(passwordGuessHash) {
    callback(passwordHash === passwordGuessHash);
  }
}
```

This approach is more verbose, but it reads more clearly and is much easier to extend. Because we've given the async result (passwordHash) broader scope, we have more flexibility.

As a rule, *avoid more than two levels of function nesting.* The key is to figure out a way of storing async results outside of the function making the async call so that the callback doesn't have to be nested.

If all of this sounds tricky, don't worry. We'll see plenty of examples in later chapters of async events running in sequence without nested handlers.

1.6 What We've Learned

In this chapter, we've seen how JavaScript's single-threadedness is both a blessing and a curse. In the right hands, it makes for beautiful code free of the terrifying race conditions that plague multithreaded apps. But you need to develop the right mind-set—and the right techniques.

The rest of this book is concerned with libraries and design patterns for working with events in JavaScript. All of the examples we'll look at will run in either mainstream browsers or unmodified Node.js. However, writing JavaScript isn't the only way to produce JavaScript code. For an overview of some interesting alternatives, see Appendix 1, *Tools for Taming JavaScript*, on page 81.

It bears mention here that there is one kind of multithreading in JavaScript: you can spawn worker processes. Each spawned process can exchange data with other processes under the same limitations as any other I/O. Workers make it possible to utilize multiple cores, without breaking the rules of JavaScript (code can't be interrupted; variables are accessible only within their scope). For more on workers, skip ahead to Chapter 5, *Multithreading with Workers*, on page 61.

The next two chapters are devoted to essential design patterns: PubSub, a way of organizing callbacks by assigning them to named events; and Promises, an intuitive object representation for one-shot events.

CHAPTER 2

Distributing Events

In the previous chapter, we looked at how async events work in JavaScript. But in practice, how should we handle those events?

That may sound like a silly question. Just attach a handler to each event your app cares about, right? But when a single event has several consequences, the "one event, one handler" approach forces handlers to grow to *gargantuan* proportions.

Let's say you're building a web-based word processor like Google Docs. Every time a user presses a key, a number of things need to happen: the new character has to be displayed on the screen, the caret has to be moved, the action has to be pushed to the local undo history and synced to the server, spell-check may have to run, and the word count and page count may need to be updated. Carrying out all of these tasks and more from a single keypress handler is a daunting proposition.

From a purely mechanical perspective, every task that we want performed in response to the event does indeed have to be initiated from its handler. But for the sake of us humans, it's usually better to replace that massive event handler with a more malleable, dynamic construct—one that we can add tasks to, and remove tasks from, at runtime. In short, we want to use *distributed events*, where a single incident can trigger reactions throughout our application.

In this chapter, you'll learn to distribute events using the publish/subscribe pattern (aka *PubSub*). Along the way, we'll meet several of PubSub's manifestations: Node's EventEmitter, Backbone's evented models, and jQuery's custom events. With the help of these tools, we'll be able to un-nest callbacks, reduce duplication, and write event-driven code that's easy to understand.

2.1 PubSub

Since the dawn of JavaScript, browsers have allowed event handlers to be attached to DOM elements like so:

```
link.onclick = clickHandler;
```

Ah, simplicity itself! There's just one caveat: if you wanted *two* click handlers for an element, you'd have to aggregate them yourself with a wrapper function.

```
link.onclick = function() {
  clickHandler1.apply(this, arguments);
  clickHandler2.apply(this, arguments);
};
```

Not only is this tedious, it's also a recipe for bloated, all-purpose handler functions. That's why the W3C added addEventListener to the DOM specification in 2000 and jQuery abstracted it with the bind method. bind makes it easy to add as many handlers as you like to any event on any element (or set of elements), without worrying about stepping on anyone else's toes.

```
$(link)
  .bind('click', clickHandler1)
  .bind('click', clickHandler2);
```

(In jQuery 1.7+, the new on syntax is preferred over bind.[1] There's also the click method, which is a shorthand for bind('click', ...); however, I prefer to consistently use bind/on.)

From a software architecture perspective, jQuery *publishes* the link element's events to anyone who wants to *subscribe*. That's why it's called "PubSub."

The old-style DOM event API, where binding to event meant writing object.onevent = ..., is now largely forgotten in favor of PubSub. The architects of Node's API liked PubSub so much that they decided to include a generic PubSub entity called EventEmitter that other objects can inherit from. Just about every source of I/O in Node is an EventEmitter: file streams, HTTP servers, and even the application process itself. To wit:

Distributed/processExit.js
```
['room', 'moon', 'cow jumping over the moon']
.forEach(function(name) {
  process.on('exit', function() {
    console.log('Goodnight, ' + name);
  });
});
```

---

1.   http://api.jquery.com/on/

Countless stand-alone PubSub libraries exist for the browser. In addition, many MVC frameworks like Backbone.js and Spine provide their own EventEmitter-like modules. We'll talk more about Backbone later in this chapter.

EventEmitter

Let's use Node's EventEmitter as an example of a PubSub interface. It has a simple, nearly minimal design.

To add an event handler to an EventEmitter, just call on with the event type and the handler.

```
emitter.on('evacuate', function(message) {
  console.log(message);
});
```

The emit method will call all handlers for the given event type. For instance, the following

```
emitter.emit('evacuate');
```

would call all evacuate handlers.

Note that the term *event* here has nothing to do with the event queue. See *Synchronicity*, on page 22.

You can add any number of additional arguments when you emit an event. All arguments are passed to all handlers.

```
emitter.emit('evacuate', 'Woman and children first!');
```

There are no restrictions on event names, though the Node docs offer a useful convention.

Typically, event names are represented by a camel-cased string.[2]

All of EventEmitter's methods are public, but it's common convention for events to be emitted only from "inside" the EventEmitter. That is, if you have an object that inherits the EventEmitter prototype and uses this.emit to broadcast events, its emit method shouldn't be called elsewhere.

Roll Your Own PubSub

PubSub implementations are so simple that we can create one in about a dozen lines of code. The only state we need to store is a list of handlers for each event type we support.

```
PubSub = {handlers: {}}
```

---

2. http://nodejs.org/docs/latest/api/events.html

When we add a listener, we push it to the end of the array (which means that listeners will always be called in the order in which they were added).

```
PubSub.on = function(eventType, handler) {
  if (!(eventType in this.handlers)) {
    this.handlers[eventType] = [];
  }

  this.handlers[eventType].push(handler);
  return this;
}
```

Then when an event is emitted, we loop through all of our handlers.

```
PubSub.emit = function(eventType) {
  var handlerArgs = Array.prototype.slice.call(arguments, 1);
  for (var i = 0; i < this.handlers[eventType].length; i++) {
    this.handlers[eventType][i].apply(this, handlerArgs);
  }
  return this;
}
```

That's it. We've just implemented the core of Node's EventEmitter. (The only major things we're missing are the ability to remove handlers and to attach one-time handlers.)

Of course, PubSub implementations vary slightly feature-wise. When the jQuery team noticed that several different PubSub implementations were being used throughout the library, they decided to abstract them with $.Callbacks in jQuery 1.7.[3] Instead of using an array to store the handlers corresponding to an event type, you could use a $.Callbacks instance.

Many PubSub implementations parse the event string to provide special features. For example, you may be familiar with namespaced events in jQuery: if I bind events named "click.tbb" and "hover.tbb", I can unbind them both by simply calling unbind(".tbb"). Backbone.js lets you bind handlers to the "all" event type, causing them to go off whenever anything happens. Both jQuery and Backbone let you bind or emit multiple event types simultaneously by separating them with spaces, e.g., "keypress mousemove".

Synchronicity

Although PubSub is an important technique for dealing with async events, there's nothing inherently async about it. Consider this code:

---

3. http://api.jquery.com/jQuery.Callbacks/

```
$('input[type=submit]')
.on('click', function() { console.log('foo'); })
.trigger('click');
console.log('bar');
```

The output is

```
‹ foo
bar
```

proving that the click handler was invoked immediately by trigger. In fact, whenever a jQuery event fires, all of its handlers will be executed sequentially without interruption.

So, let's be clear: when the user clicks the Submit button, that's an async event. The first click handler fires from the event queue. But the event handler has no way of knowing whether it's being run from the event queue or from your application code.

If too many handlers fire in sequence, you risk blocking the thread and making the browser unresponsive. Worse, if events are emitted from event handlers, they can easily create an infinite cycle.

```
$('input[type=submit]')
.on('click', function() {
  $(this).trigger('click');  // stack overflow!
});
```

Think back to the word processor example at the start of this chapter. When a user presses a key, many things need to happen, and several of them require complex calculations. Doing them all before returning to the event queue would be a recipe for an unresponsive app.

A good solution to this problem is to maintain a queue of things that don't need to happen right away and use a timed function to run the next task in the queue periodically. A first attempt might look something like this:

```
var tasks = [];
setInterval(function() {
  var nextTask;
  if (nextTask = tasks.shift()) {
    nextTask();
  };
}, 0);
```

(We'll learn about a more sophisticated approach to job queuing in Section 4.4, *Dynamic Async Queuing*, on page 54.)

PubSub makes it easy to name, distribute, and stack events. Anytime it makes intuitive sense for an object to announce that something has happened, PubSub is a great pattern to use.

2.2 Evented Models

When an object has a PubSub interface, we call it an *evented object*. A special case is when an object used to store data (a *model*) publishes events whenever its contents are modified. Models are the *M* in Model-View-Controller (MVC), which has become one of the hottest topics in JavaScript programming in the last few years. The core concept is that MVC applications are data-centric so that model events impact the DOM (aka the View) and the server (via the Controller).

Let's look at the hugely popular Backbone.js framework.[4] You create a new model like so:

```
style = new Backbone.Model(
  {font: 'Georgia'}
);
```

model just represents the simple object that was passed in.

```
style.toJSON()  // {"font": "Georgia"}
```

But unlike an ordinary object, this one publishes notifications when a change is made.

```
style.on('change:font', function(model, font) {
  alert('Thank you for choosing ' + font + '!');
});
```

Old-school JavaScript made changes to the DOM directly from input event handlers. New-school JavaScript makes changes to models, which then emit events that cause the DOM to update. In nearly all apps, this separation of concerns results in more elegant, intuitive code.

Propagating Model Events

In its simplest form, MVC consists of wiring models to views: "If this model changes this way, change the DOM that way." But the biggest gains from MVC happen when change events bubble up the data tree. Instead of subscribing to events on every leaf, you can just subscribe to the roots and branches.

---

4.   http://documentcloud.github.com/backbone/

Set/Get on Evented Models

JavaScript as we know it doesn't have a mechanism for firing an event every time an object is modified. So, for evented models to work, we have to remember to use methods like Backbone's set and get.

```
style.set({font: 'Palatino'});    // triggers alert!
style.get('font');                // "Palatino"
style.font = 'Comic Sans';        // no events fire
style.font;                       // "Comic Sans"
style.get('font');                // Still "Palatino"
```

This may not be necessary in the future, if an ECMAScript proposal called Object.observe becomes widely adopted.[a]

---

a.   https://plus.google.com/111386188573471152118/posts/6peb6yffyWG

To that end, Backbone models are often organized into Backbone collections, which are essentially evented arrays. You can listen for when models are added to and removed from them. Backbone collections automatically propagate events from the models they contain.

For example, you might have a spriteCollection object containing hundreds of models representing things you're drawing on a canvas element. Each time any of those sprites change, you need to redraw the canvas. Rather than attaching the redraw function as a handler for the change event on each sprite individually, you could instead just write the following:

```
spriteCollection.on('change', redraw);
```

Note that this automatic propagation goes only one level down. Backbone has no notion of nested collections. However, you can implement this propagation yourself using Backbone's trigger method. With it, any Backbone object can emit arbitrary events.

Cycles and Nested Changes

Propagating events from one object to another poses certain concerns. If an event on one object causes a series of events that will ultimately trigger the same event on the same object every time, then the result will be an event cycle. And if the cycle is synchronous, the result will be a stack overflow, like we saw in *Synchronicity*, on page 22.

Yet oftentimes, a cycle of change events is exactly what we want. The most common case is a *two-way binding*, where two models have interrelated values. Suppose we want to ensure that x always equals 2 * y.

```
var x = new Backbone.Model({value: 0});
var y = new Backbone.Model({value: 0});
x.on('change:value', function(x, xVal) { y.set({value: xVal / 2}); });
y.on('change:value', function(y, yVal) { x.set({value: 2 * yVal}); });
```

You might expect this code to lead to an infinite loop the moment the value of x or y is changed. But actually, it's quite safe, thanks to two safeguards in Backbone.

- set doesn't emit a change event if the new value matches the old one.
- Models can't emit a change event during one of its own change events.

The second safeguard presents gotchas of its own. Suppose a change is made to a model that results in a second change to the same model. Because the second change is "nested" in the first one, it'll occur silently. Observers won't have a chance to respond to it.

Clearly, maintaining two-way data bindings in Backbone is a challenge. Another major MVC framework, Ember.js, takes a different approach: two-way bindings are declared explicitly. When one value changes, the other is updated asynchronously from a timeout event. So, until that event fires, the application's data may be in an inconsistent state.

There's no easy solution to the problem of bindings across evented models. In Backbone, a prudent way to step around the issue is the silent flag. If you add {silent: true} to a set event, no change event will happen. So, if several entangled models need to be updated at once, a good approach is to set them silently. Then call their change methods to fire the appropriate events only after they're in a consistent state.

Evented models give us an intuitive way of transforming application state changes into events. Everything Backbone and other MVC frameworks do is about these models, updating the DOM and the server when their states change. Storing mutable data in evented models is a great first step to reigning in the growing complexity of client-side JavaScript applications.

2.3 Custom jQuery Events

Custom events are an underappreciated feature of jQuery that make it easy to graft a powerful distributed event system onto any web app, with no additional libraries. You can emit any event you want from any DOM element from jQuery using trigger.

```
$('#tabby, #socks').on('meow', function() {
  console.log(this.id + ' meowed');
});
$('#tabby').trigger('meow');  // "tabby meowed"
$('#socks').trigger('meow');  // "socks meowed"
```

If you've worked with DOM events before, you're no doubt familiar with *bubbling*. Whenever an element emits an event (such as a 'click'), its parent then emits the event, then its grandparent, and so on, up to the root element, document—unless the event's stopPropagation method is called at some point along the way. (jQuery does this for us automatically when we return false from a handler.) But did you know that jQuery's custom events bubble as well? For instance, if we have a span named "soda" nested in a div named "bottle," the code

```
$('#soda, #bottle').on('fizz', function() {
  console.log(this.id + ' emitted fizz');
});
$('#soda').trigger('fizz');
```

will emit the following output:

```
soda emitted fizz
bottle emitted fizz
```

This bubbling isn't always desirable, as we'll see in the following tooltips example. Fortunately, jQuery offers the nonbubbling triggerHandler method as well.

Example: Tooltips

When events can be mapped intuitively to page elements, jQuery is an ideal way of distributing them. For instance, suppose you're writing a tooltip library and you want only one tooltip to be visible at a time. You might simply add the line

```
$('.tooltip').remove();
```

to the start of the function that adds new tooltips. But what if we decide later that we want certain containers to be isolated, such as when a new tooltip is shown in the sidebar, tooltips everywhere else are unaffected, and vice versa? Writing a selector for "elements with class tooltip that are *not* descendants of sidebar" is tricky and not very efficient. The problem would get exponentially harder if we decided to allow isolated containers to be nested to an arbitrary depth.

But implementing this behavior with event logic rather than selector logic is easy.

```
// $container could be $('#sidebar') or $(document)
$container.triggerHandler('newTooltip');
$container.one('newTooltip', function() {
  $tooltip.remove();
});
```

(Notice the use of jQuery's one instead of on. The difference is that one automatically removes the handler after it fires.)

With these two lines of code, each tooltip will listen to its container and remove itself when the container gets a new tooltip. It's a beautifully direct, efficient approach that saves us from having to store any state or engineer complex selectors (which would slow older browsers to a crawl—IE7 and older don't even have a way of selecting all elements with the tooltip class without traversing the whole document!).

Note that event bubbling would actually have defeated our intent in this case: when we create a new tooltip in the sidebar, we want only tooltips listening for the 'newTooltip' event on the sidebar itself to go away, not those on the surrounding document. Always think carefully about whether trigger or triggerHandler is the right tool for the job.

Custom jQuery events are an unusual twist on PubSub, since the events are emitted by selectable elements rather than by objects in our script. Much as evented models are an intuitive way of expressing state-related events, jQuery events let us express DOM-related events directly through the DOM, saving us from having to duplicate that state elsewhere in our application. Use them liberally, but try to avoid relying on the structure of your application's markup —you don't want your next redesign to break your script.

2.4 What We've Learned

In this chapter, we've learned about distributing events via PubSub, one of the most fundamental JavaScript design patterns. When you're not subscribing to the events that are being published, PubSub is completely unobtrusive. The key to using PubSub properly is deciding which entities to distribute events through.

We've seen that any object can be used for PubSub, simply by inheriting from something like Node's EventEmitter. Whenever an object is associated with a set of async tasks or I/O events, it's a good idea to make it evented.

One class of evented object is the models in MVC libraries like Backbone.js. These models both contain application state and announce changes to it. Change events can trigger application logic, DOM updates, and synchronization with the server. It all feels very natural, which explains why Backbone has become a smash-hit library.

We've also seen that jQuery is great for distributing events related to changes in the DOM, not just the DOM events provided by the browser. Evented objects and DOM events complement each other perfectly, helping to keep the application's state and view encapsulated from each other.

All of these are examples of PubSub in action. However, as versatile as it is, PubSub isn't the right tool for every job. In particular, it's a poor fit for one-shot events, when an async function performs a task whose completion or failure needs to be handled in a unique way. (An Ajax request is a common example.) One tool for solving that problem, called a *Promise*, is the subject of the next chapter.

CHAPTER 3

Promises and Deferreds

In 2010, I had this conversation with my prolific colleague Mr. Ajax:

> **Me:** *Hey, would you fetch some data from this URL for me, please?*
>
> **Mr. Ajax:** *I'm on it! Just give me a success callback so I can let you know when I'm done.*
>
> **Me:** *OK, here you go. Thanks.*
>
> **Mr. Ajax:** *Oh, and you should give me an error callback, too. You know, just in case.*
>
> **Me:** *Good point. Anything else?*
>
> **Mr. Ajax:** *Hey, I noticed that there's some code duplication between those two callbacks! You could move that into a third always callback.*
>
> **Me:** *(impatiently) Alright, I'll refactor them. Tell you what: why don't you run now, and I'll give you the callbacks later?*
>
> **Mr. Ajax:** *(irately) What do I look like, an EventEmitter?*

Thankfully, jQuery 1.5 changed Mr. Ajax's need-it-now attitude. All of the Ajax functions you know and love ($.ajax, $.get, and $.post) now return Promises. A *Promise* is an object that represents a task with two possible outcomes (success or failure) and holds callbacks that fire when one outcome or the other has occurred. For example, under jQuery 1.4, I'd have had to write this:

Promises/get-1.4.js
```
$.get('/mydata', {
  success: onSuccess,
  failure: onFailure,
  always: onAlways
});
```

But under jQuery 1.5+, I can write this instead:

Promises/get-1.5.js

```
var promise = $.get('/mydata');
promise.done(onSuccess);
promise.fail(onFailure);
promise.always(onAlways);
```

You might wonder what's so great about this change. Why would you want to attach a callback after an Ajax call has fired? In a word: *encapsulation.* If an Ajax call has multiple effects (triggering animations, inserting HTML, locking/unlocking user input, and so on), it's awkward for the part of your app that's making the request to handle all of them.

It's much more elegant to pass a Promise around. By passing a Promise, you're announcing, "Something you might be interested in is happening. If you want to find out when it's done, just give this Promise a callback." And like an EventEmitter, a Promise allows you to bind handlers to the same event as many times as you like (*stacking*). That makes it a lot easier to reduce code duplication when some small piece of functionality (like a "Loading" animation) is shared across several Ajax calls.

But the biggest advantage of using Promises is that you can easily derive new Promises from existing ones. You might ask two Promises representing parallel tasks to give you a Promise that will inform you of their mutual completion. Or you might ask a Promise representing the first task in a series to give you a Promise representing the *final* task in the series. As we'll soon see, these operations come naturally with Promises.

3.1 A Very Brief History of Promises

Promises have existed in many forms in many languages. The term was first used by C++ engineers on the Xanadu project, a forerunner to the Web. Promises were later used in the E programming language, which inspired Python developers to implement them in the form of the Twisted framework's Deferreds.

Promises hit the JavaScript mainstream in 2007 when the Dojo framework, taking a cue from Twisted, added an object called dojo.Deferred. At the time, the relatively mature Dojo rivaled the fledgling jQuery framework in popularity. In 2009, citing dojo.Deferred as an influence, Kris Zyp proposed the CommonJS Promises/A spec.[1] That same year, Node.js made its first appearance. Node's early iterations used Promises in its nonblocking API. However, in February 2010, Ryan Dahl made the decision to switch to the

---

1. http://wiki.commonjs.org/wiki/Promises/A

now-familiar callback(err, results...) format, on the grounds that Promises are a higher-level construct that belongs in "userland."

This decision made way for competing Promises implementations aimed at Node, notably Kris Kowal's Q.js[2] and AJ ONeal's Futures.[3] (In common usage, the terms *Promise*, *Deferred*, and *Future* are roughly synonymous.) Q is a fairly straightforward implementation of the Promises/A spec. Futures is a broader toolkit, incorporating many of the flow control features found in libraries like Async.js.

But the reason Promises are getting so much attention today is, of course, jQuery. Accompanying a major rewrite of $.ajax in January 2011, jQuery 1.5's Promises implementation thrilled countless developers who were encountering Promises for the first time. Others, however, were frustrated that the Promises/A spec had been ignored, leading to subtle API differences.

We'll focus on jQuery Promises for the rest of this chapter, except in Section 3.7, *jQuery vs. Promises/A*, on page 43. We'll also take our vocabulary cues from jQuery, particularly the distinction between Deferreds and Promises that we'll see in the next section and the use of "resolve" as the antonym of "reject."

3.2 Making Promises

We started this chapter by showing how the Ajax methods in jQuery 1.5+ ($.ajax, $.get, and $.post) return Promises. But to really understand Promises, we need to make a few of our own.

Let's give the user a prompt to hit either Y or N. The first thing we'll do is create an instance of $.Deferred that represents the user's decision.

```
var promptDeferred = new $.Deferred();
promptDeferred.always(function(){ console.log('A choice was made:'); });
promptDeferred.done(function(){ console.log('Starting game...'); });
promptDeferred.fail(function(){ console.log('No game today.'); });
```

(Note: always is available only in jQuery 1.6+.)

You're probably wondering why I created an instance of Deferred when this section is called "Making Promises." Fear not—a Deferred *is* a Promise! More precisely, it's a superset of Promise with one critical addition: *you can trigger a Deferred directly.* A pure Promise only lets you add more callbacks; someone else has to trigger them.

---

2. https://github.com/kriskowal/q
3. https://github.com/coolaj86/futures

We can trigger our Deferred with the resolve and reject methods.

```
$('#playGame').focus().on('keypress', function(e) {
  var Y = 121, N = 110;
  if (e.keyCode === Y) {
    promptDeferred.resolve();
  } else if (e.keyCode === N) {
    promptDeferred.reject();
  } else {
    return false;  // our Deferred remains pending
  };
});
```

You can see this example in action at http://jsfiddle.net/TrevorBurnham/PJ6Bf/. Load the page and hit Y. The console will say the following:

```
❮ A choice was made:
Starting game...
```

You see what happened? When the Deferred was resolved, its always and done callbacks were run. (Not coincidentally, the callbacks were run in the order in which they were bound.)

Refresh the page and hit N.

```
❮ A choice was made:
No game today.
```

So, when the Deferred was rejected, its always and fail callbacks were run. Note that callbacks always run in the order in which they were bound. If the always callback had been bound last, the order of the console output would be reversed.

Try hitting Y and N repeatedly. After the first choice is made, there's no effect! That's because a Promise can be resolved or rejected only *once*; after that, it's inert. We say that a Promise is *pending* until it's either resolved or rejected. You can find out whether a Promise is "pending", "resolved", or "rejected" by calling its state method. (state was added in jQuery 1.7; in earlier versions, use isResolved and isRejected.)

When you're carrying out a one-shot async operation with two broad outcomes (e.g., success/failure or accept/decline), making a Deferred gives you an intuitive representation of it.

Making a Pure Promise

We just learned that a Deferred is a Promise. So, how do we get a Promise that isn't a Deferred? Simple: call a Deferred's promise method.

> ## A Tale of Two Terminologies
>
> You might have noticed that I've been saying that I "trigger" a Promise when I resolve or reject it and that a Promise that's been resolved or rejected has been "triggered." This is a nonstandard term, but I'll be using it throughout this chapter. jQuery, unfortunately, lacks a succinct term for a Promise that's been either resolved or rejected, other than the cumbersome "nonpending."
>
> A more sensible terminology is used in the Promises/A spec and its implementations: a Promise is either *fulfilled* or rejected; either way, it's resolved. We'll learn more about that in Section 3.7, *jQuery vs. Promises/A*, on page 43.

```
var promptPromise = promptDeferred.promise();
```

promptPromise is just a copy of promptDeferred without the resolve/reject methods. It doesn't matter whether we bind a callback to a Deferred or to its Promise, because they share the same callbacks internally. They also share the same state ("pending", "resolved", or "rejected"). This means that creating multiple Promises for a single Deferred would be pointless. In fact, jQuery will just give you the same object.

```
var promise1 = promptDeferred.promise();
var promise2 = promptDeferred.promise();
console.log(promise1 === promise2);  // true
```

And calling promise on a pure Promise just gives you a reference to the same object.

```
console.log(promise1 === promise1.promise());  // true
```

The only reason to use the promise method is encapsulation. If we pass promptPromise around but keep promptDeferred to ourselves, we can rest assured that none of our callbacks will fire until we want them to fire.

To reiterate, every Deferred contains a Promise, and every Promise represents a Deferred. When you have a Deferred, you control its state. When you have a pure Promise, you can only read that state and attach callbacks.

Promises in the jQuery API

I started the chapter with the example of Promises returned by jQuery's Ajax functions ($.ajax, $.get, and $.post). Ajax is a perfect use case for Promises: every call to a remote server will either succeed or fail, and you'll want to handle those cases differently. But Promises can be just as useful for local async operations, like animations.

In jQuery, you can pass a callback to any animation method to be notified when it's finished.

```
$('.error').fadeIn(afterErrorShown);
```

In jQuery 1.6+, you can instead ask a jQuery object for a Promise, which represents the completion of its current and pending animations.

```
var errorPromise = $('.error').fadeIn().promise();
errorPromise.done(afterErrorShown);
```

Animations applied to the same jQuery object are queued to run sequentially, and the Promise resolves only when all animations that were on the queue when you called promise were resolved. So, this generates two distinct Promises that will be resolved in sequence (or not at all, if stop is called first).

```
var $flash = $('.flash');
var showPromise = $flash.show();
var hidePromise = $flash.hide();
```

Pretty simple, right? In jQuery 1.6 and 1.7, a promise on a jQuery object is just a convenience method. You could easily create an animation Promise with the same behavior yourself by using a Deferred's resolve method as the animation callback.

```
var slideUpDeferred = new $.Deferred();
$('.menu').slideUp(slideUpDeferred.resolve);
var slideUpPromise = slideUpDeferred.promise();
```

In jQuery 1.8, released shortly before this book went to press, animation Promises have become much more powerful objects. The Promise has additional information attached, including props, the computed values that the animation is moving toward—very valuable for debugging. You can also get progress notifications (see Section 3.4, *Progress Notifications*, on page 38) and adjust the animation on the fly. Draft documentation for this new set of features can be found at https://gist.github.com/54829d408993526fe475.

jQuery 1.8 added one more source of Promises in jQuery: $.ready.promise() gives you a Promise that resolves when the document is ready. That means that these are now equivalent:

```
$(onReady);
 $(document).ready(onReady);
 $.ready.promise().done(onReady);
```

In this section, we've seen how you obtain jQuery Promises: either you create a $.Deferred instance, giving you a Promise that you control, or you make an

API call that returns a Promise. In the next few sections, we'll see what you can do with all those Promises.

3.3 Passing Data to Callbacks

A Promise can give its callbacks additional information. For example, these two Ajax snippets are equivalent:

```
// Using a callback directly
$.get(url, successCallback);

// Binding a callback to a Promise
var fetchingData = $.get(url);
fetchingData.done(successCallback);
```

When you resolve or reject a Deferred, any arguments you provide are relayed to the corresponding callbacks.

```
var aDreamDeferred = new $.Deferred();
aDreamDeferred.done(function(subject) {
  console.log('I had the most wonderful dream about', subject);
});
aDreamDeferred.resolve('the JS event model');
```

❮ I had the most wonderful dream about the JS event model

There are also special methods for running the callbacks in a particular context (that is, setting this to a particular value): resolveWith and rejectWith. Just pass the context as the first argument, and pass all other arguments in as an array.

```
var slashdotter = {
  comment: function(editor){
    console.log('Obviously', editor, 'is the best text editor.');
  }
};
var grammarDeferred = new $.Deferred();
grammarDeferred.done(function(verb, object) {
  this[verb](object);
});
grammarDeferred.resolveWith(slashdotter, ['comment', 'Emacs']);
```

❮ Obviously Emacs is the best text editor.

Having to wrap your arguments in an array is a pain, though. So, here's a handy tip: instead of using resolveWith/rejectWith, you can just invoke plain resolve/reject in the desired context. That's because resolve/reject pass their context right to the callbacks they fire. So, in the previous example, we could achieve the same result with the following:

```
grammarDeferred.resolve.call(slashdotter, 'comment', 'Emacs');
```

3.4 Progress Notifications

A Promise is a bundle of things you want to happen when a process comes to an end. But didn't a motivational poster once tell you that the journey is as important as the destination? Did you learn *nothing* from that poster?

Fortunately, the jQuery team soaked up that wisdom (and the Promises/A specification) and, in jQuery 1.7, added a new kind of Promise callback that can be invoked any number of times. It's called progress. For example, suppose we want to update an indicator of how far a person has gotten toward their daily word goal for National Novel Writing Month (NaNoWriMo).[4]

```
var nanowrimoing = $.Deferred();
var wordGoal = 5000;
nanowrimoing.progress(function(wordCount) {
  var percentComplete = Math.floor(wordCount / wordGoal * 100);
  $('#indicator').text(percentComplete + '% complete');
});
nanowrimoing.done(function(){
  $('#indicator').text('Good job!');
});
```

With the nanowrimoing Deferred available, here's how we respond to potential changes in word count:

```
$('#document').on('keypress', function(){
  var wordCount = $(this).val().split(/\s+/).length;
  if (wordCount >= wordGoal) {
    nanowrimoing.resolve();
  };
  nanowrimoing.notify(wordCount);
});
```

The notify call on the Deferred invokes our progress callback. Just like resolve and reject, notify can take arbitrary arguments. Note that calls to nanowrimoing.notify will have no effect once nanowrimoing is resolved, just like any additional resolve and reject calls would be ignored.

So, to recap, a Promise takes three kinds of callbacks: done, fail, and progress. done callbacks run when the Promise resolves, fail callbacks run when it's rejected, and progress callbacks run whenever notify is called on a pending Deferred.

---

4.   http://www.nanowrimo.org/

3.5   Combining Promises

The existence of progress notifications doesn't change the fact that, ultimately, every Promise is either resolved or rejected. (Or, it remains pending for eternity.) But why? Why not let Promises change to any state at any time?

Mainly, Promises are designed this way because programmers *thrive* on binary. We know exactly how to put 1s and 0s together to perform astounding feats of logic. That's a big reason why Promises are so powerful; they let us treat tasks as booleans.

The most common use case for logically combining Promises is finding out when a set of async tasks has finished. Let's say you're showing a tutorial video while loading a game from the server. You want to start the game as soon as two things have happened, in any order.

- The tutorial video has ended.
- The game is loaded.

Given a Promise representing each of these processes, your task is to start the game when both Promises are resolved. How would you do that?

Enter jQuery's when method.

```
var gameReadying = $.when(tutorialPromise, gameLoadedPromise);
gameReadying.done(startGame);
```

when acts as a logical AND for Promise resolution. The Promise it generates is resolved as soon as all of the given Promises are resolved, or it is rejected as soon as any one of the given Promises is rejected.

An excellent use case for when is combining multiple Ajax calls. If you need to make two POST calls at once and get a notification when both have succeeded, there's no need to define a separate callback for each request.

```
$.when($.post('/1', data1), $.post('/2', data2))
.then(onPosted, onFailure);
```

On success, when can get access to the callback arguments from each of its constituent Promises, but doing so is tricky. They're passed as an argument list with the same order that the Promises were given to when. If a Promise provides multiple callback arguments, those arguments are converted to an array.

So, to get all of the callback arguments from all of the Promises given to $.when, you might write something like this (though I don't recommend it):

```
$.when(promise1, promise2)
.done(function(promise1Args, promise2Args) {
  // ...
});
```

In this example, if promise1 resolved with the single argument 'complete' and promise2 resolved with the arguments 1, 2, 3, then promise1Args would just be the string 'complete', while promise2Args would be the array [1, 2, 3].

Although it's possible, you shouldn't parse when callback arguments if you don't absolutely have to do so. Instead, attach callbacks directly to the Promises passed to when to collect their results.

```
var serverData = {};
var getting1 = $.get('/1')
.done(function(result) {serverData['1'] = result;});
var getting2 = $.get('/2')
.done(function(result) {serverData['2'] = result;});
$.when(getting1, getting2)
.done(function() {
  // the GET information is now in serverData...
});
```

Using Functions as Promises

$.when, and other jQuery methods that take Promises, allow you to pass in non-Promises. These are treated like Promises that have resolved with the given value in the corresponding argument slot. For instance,

```
$.when('foo')
```

will give you a Promise that immediately resolves with the value 'foo'; the following

```
var promise = $.Deferred().resolve('manchu');
$.when('foo', promise)
```

will give you a Promise that immediately resolves with the values 'foo' and 'manchu'; and the following

```
var promise = $.Deferred().resolve(1, 2, 3);
$.when('test', promise)
```

will give you a Promise that immediately resolves with the values 'test' and [1, 2, 3]. (Remember, when a Deferred passes multiple arguments to resolve, those arguments are coerced to an array by $.when.)

This raises the following question: how does $.when know whether an argument is a Promise? It turns out that jQuery checks each argument for a method named promise; if one exists, jQuery uses the value returned by that method. A Promise's promise method simply returns itself.

As you'll recall from *Promises in the jQuery API*, on page 35, jQuery objects also have a promise method, which means that $.when "coerces" jQuery objects into their animation Promises. So, if we want to create a Promise that will resolve when we've fetched some data and the #loading animation has completed, all we have to do is write this:

```
var fetching = $.get('/myData');
$.when(fetching, $('#loading'));
```

Just remember that we have to do this *after* starting the animation. If #loading's animation queue is empty, its Promise resolves immediately.

3.6 Binding to the Future with pipe

A big reason why performing a series of async tasks is often inconvenient in JavaScript is that you can't attach handlers to the second task until the first one is complete. As an example, let's GET data from one URL and then POST it to another.

```
var getPromise = $.get('/query');
getPromise.done(function(data) {
  var postPromise = $.post('/search', data);
});
// Now we'd like to attach handlers to postPromise...
```

Do you see what the problem is here? We can't bind callbacks to postPromise until our GET operation is done, because it doesn't exist yet! It's created by a $.post call that we can't make until we have the data that we're getting asynchronously from the $.get call.

That's why jQuery 1.6 added the pipe method to Promises. Essentially, pipe says this: "Give me a callback for this Promise, and I'll give you a Promise that represents the result of that callback."

```
var getPromise = $.get('/query');
var postPromise = getPromise.pipe(function(data) {
  return $.post('/search', data);
});
```

Looks like dark magic, right? Here's a breakdown: pipe takes one argument for each type of callback: done, fail, and progress. So, in this example, we just provided a callback that gets run when getPromise is resolved. The pipe method returns a new Promise that's resolved/rejected when the Promise returned from our callback is resolved/rejected.

Effectively, *pipe is a window into the future!*

You can also use pipe to "filter" a Promise by modifying callback arguments. If a pipe callback returns something other than a Promise/Deferred, then that value becomes the callback argument. For instance, if you have a Promise that emits progress notifications with a number between 0 and 1, you can use pipe to create an identical Promise that emits progress notifications with a human-readable string instead.

```
var promise2 = promise1.pipe(null, null, function(progress) {
  return Math.floor(progress * 100) + '% complete';
});
```

To summarize, there are two things you can do from a pipe callback.

- If you return a Promise, the Promise returned by pipe will mimic it.

- If you return a non-Promise value (or nothing), the Promise returned by pipe will immediately be resolved, rejected, or notified with that value, according to what just happened to the original Promise.

pipe's rule for whether something is a Promise is the same as $.when's: if it has a promise method, that method's return value is used as a Promise representing the original object. Again, promise.promise() === promise.

Pipe Cascading

pipe doesn't require you to provide every possible callback. In fact, you'll usually just want to write

```
var pipedPromise = originalPromise.pipe(successCallback);
```

or the following:

```
var pipedPromise = originalPromise.pipe(null, failCallback);
```

We've seen what happens when the original Promise succeeds in the first case, or fails in the second case, so that the piped Promise's behavior depends on the return value of successCallback or failCallback. But what about when we haven't given pipe a callback for what the original Promise does?

It's simple. The piped Promise mimics the original Promise in those cases. We can say that the original Promise's behavior *cascades* through the piped Promise. This cascading is very handy, because it allows us to define branching logic for async tasks with minimal effort. Suppose we have a three-step process.

```
var step1 = $.post('/step1', data1);
var step2 = step1.pipe(function() {
  return $.post('/step2', data2);
});
var lastStep = step2.pipe(function() {
  return $.post('/step3', data3);
});
```

Here, lastStep will resolve only if all three Ajax calls succeeded, and it'll be rejected if *any* of the three fail. If we care only about the process as a whole, we can omit the variable declarations for the earlier steps.

```
var posting = $.post('/step1', data1)
  .pipe(function() {
    return $.post('/step2', data2);
  })
    .pipe(function() {
      return $.post('/step3', data3);
    });
```

We could, equivalently, nest the second pipe inside of the other.

```
var posting = $.post('/step1', data1)
  .pipe(function() {
    return $.post('/step2', data2)
    .pipe(function() {
      return $.post('/step3', data3);
    });
  });
```

Of course, this brings us back to the Pyramid of Doom. You should be aware of this style, but as a rule, try to declare your piped Promises individually. The variable names may not be necessary, but they make the code far more self-documenting.

That concludes our tour of jQuery Promises. Now let's take a quick look at the major alternative: the CommonJS Promises/A specification and its flagship implementation, Q.js.

3.7 jQuery vs. Promises/A

In terms of capabilities, jQuery Promises and Promises/A are nearly identical. Q.js, the most popular Promises/A library, even offers methods that can work with jQuery Promises. The differences are superficial; they use the same words to mean different things.

As previously mentioned in Section 3.2, *Making Promises*, on page 33, jQuery uses the term *resolve* as the opposite of *fail*, whereas Promises/A uses *fulfill*.

Under Promises/A, a Promise is said to be "resolved" when it's either fulfilled or failed.

Up until the release of 1.8, jQuery's then method was just a shorthand for invoking done, fail, and progress simultaneously, while Promises/A's then acted more like jQuery's pipe. jQuery 1.8 corrected this by making then a synonym for pipe. However, any further reconciliation with Promises/A is unlikely because of backward compatibility concerns.

There are other, subtler differences as well. For instance, in Promises/A, whether a Promise returned by then is fulfilled or rejected depends on whether the invoked callback returns a value or throws an error. (Throwing errors from jQuery Promise callbacks is a bad idea because they'll go uncaught.)

Because of these issues, you should try to avoid interacting with multiple Promise implementations in the same project. If you're just getting Promises from jQuery methods, use jQuery Promises. If you're using another library that gives you CommonJS Promises, adopt Promises/A. Q.js makes it easy to "assimilate" jQuery Promises.

```
var qPromise = Q.when(jqPromise);
```

As long as these two standards remain divergent, this is the best way to make them play nice together. For more information, see the Q.js docs.[5]

3.8   Replacing Callbacks with Promises

In a perfect world, every function that started an async task would return a Promise. Unfortunately, most JavaScript APIs (including the native functions available in all browsers and in Node.js) are callback-based, not Promise-based. In this section, we'll see how Promises can be used with callback-based APIs.

The most straightforward way to use Promises with a callback-based API is to create a Deferred and pass its trigger function(s) as the callback argument(s). For example, with a simple async function like setTimeout, we'd pass our Deferred's resolve method.

```
var timing = new $.Deferred();
setTimeout(timing.resolve, 500);
```

In cases where an error could occur, we'd write a callback that conditionally routes to either resolve or reject. For example, here's how we'd work with a Node-style callback:

---

5.   https://github.com/kriskowal/q

```
var fileReading = new $.Deferred();
fs.readFile(filename, 'utf8', function(err) {
  if (err) {
    fileReading.reject(err);
  } else {
    fileReading.resolve(Array.prototype.slice.call(arguments, 1));
  };
});
```

(Yes, you can use jQuery from Node. Just npm install jquery and use it like any other module. There's also a self-contained implementation of jQuery-style Promises, simply called Standalone Deferred.[6])

Writing this out routinely would be a drag, so why not make a utility function to generate a Node-style callback from any given Deferred?

```
deferredCallback = function(deferred) {
  return function(err) {
    if (err) {
      deferred.reject(err);
    } else {
      deferred.resolve(Array.prototype.slice.call(arguments, 1));
    };
  };
}
```

With that, we can write the previous example as follows:

```
var fileReading = new $.Deferred();
fs.readFile(filename, 'utf8', deferredCallback(fileReading));
```

In Q.js, Deferreds come with a node method for this right out of the box.

```
var fileReading = Q.defer();
fs.readFile(filename, 'utf8', fileReading.node());
```

As Promises become more popular, more and more JavaScript libraries will follow jQuery's lead and return Promises from their async functions. Until then, it takes only a few lines of code to turn any async function you want to use into a Promise generator.

3.9   What We've Learned

In my opinion, Promises are one of the most exciting features to be added to jQuery in years. Not only are they a big help in smoothing out the callback spaghetti that characterizes typical Ajax-rich apps, but they also make it much easier to coordinate async tasks of all kinds.

---

6.   https://github.com/Mumakil/Standalone-Deferred

Using Promises takes some practice, especially when using pipe, but it's a habit well worth developing. You'll be peering into the future of JavaScript. The more APIs return Promises, the more compelling they become.

Microsoft has announced that Windows 8's Metro environment will have a Promise-based JavaScript API.[7] Where hipster developers and Microsoft both go, the rest of the world is bound to follow.

---

7.   http://msdn.microsoft.com/en-us/library/windows/apps/br211867.aspx

CHAPTER 4

Flow Control with Async.js

Up to this point, this book has been about using abstractions to manage async tasks throughout an application. PubSub, for instance, is an abstraction that lets us distribute events from their source to other layers of the application (e.g., from the view to the model). Promises are an abstraction that let us represent simple tasks with objects that can be combined to represent complex tasks. Together, these abstractions go a long way toward helping us solve the problem of callback spaghetti.

There's still one weak spot in our armor, though: iteration. What do we do when we need to perform a series of I/O operations, either in series or in parallel? This is such a common problem in the Node world that it has a name: *flow control* (also called *control flow*). And the same way that Underscore.js can dramatically simplify (synchronous) iterative code, a good flow control library can strip away the boilerplate from your async code.

The most popular of these libraries is Caolan McMahon's powerful Async.js.[1] In fact, as of this writing, Async.js is the third most required library in the npm registry,[2] sharing the limelight with superstars like Underscore.js and Express.

In this chapter, we'll explore what Async.js can do in a Node setting. (Async.js can run in the browser, too, but few client-side apps need it.) We'll also take a brief look at an alternative library, Tim Caswell's sleek Step.[3]

---

1. https://github.com/caolan/async
2. https://npmjs.org/
3. https://github.com/creationix/step

> ### Installing Node and Async.js
>
> To follow along with this chapter, grab the latest Node from http://nodejs.org/. After installing, you should be able to run npm, the Node package manager. Use this command to install Async.js and Step:
>
> ```
> npm install -g async step
> ```
>
> Then use node file.js to run any JavaScript file.

4.1 The Async Ordering Problem

Suppose we want to read all of the files in the recipes directory, in alphabetical order, and then concatenate their contents into a single string and display it. We could do this quite easily using synchronous methods.

```
Asyncjs/synchronous.js
var fs = require('fs');
process.chdir('recipes');  // change the working directory

var concatenation = '';

fs.readdirSync('.')
  .filter(function(filename) {
    // ignore directories
    return fs.statSync(filename).isFile();
  })
    .forEach(function(filename) {
      // add contents to our output
      concatenation += fs.readFileSync(filename, 'utf8');
    });

console.log(concatenation);
```

(Be aware that the forEach iterator isn't available in older JavaScript environments, such as IE6. You can fix this with a library like Kris Kowal's es5-shim.[4] We'll learn how to serve this library to just the browsers that need it in Chapter 6, *Async Script Loading*, on page 69.)

But all this blocking is terribly inefficient, particularly if our application could be doing something else simultaneously. The problem is that we can't just naïvely replace

```
concatenation += fs.readFileSync(filename, 'utf8');
```

with its async analog

---

4.   https://github.com/kriskowal/es5-shim/

```
fs.readFile(filename, 'utf8', function(err, contents) {
  if (err) throw err;
  concatenation += contents;
});
```

because there's no guarantee that the readFile callbacks would fire in the order that the readFile calls were made in. readFile just tells the OS to *start* reading a file. Most likely, shorter files will be read more quickly than longer files. As a result, the order in which the recipes are added to concatenation would be unpredictable. Plus, we'd have to make our console.log line somehow run after all the callbacks have fired.

To use multiple async tasks and get a predictable result, we'll need to do some planning.

4.2 Async Collection Methods

Let's try to solve this problem without bringing in any utility functions. The simplest approach that I can think of is to run each readFile from the callback of the previous one, while keeping track of the number of callbacks that have fired so far in order to eventually show the output. Here's my implementation:

```
Asyncjs/seriesByHand.js
var fs = require('fs');
process.chdir('recipes');  // change the working directory
var concatenation = '';

fs.readdir('.', function(err, filenames) {
  if (err) throw err;

  function readFileAt(i) {
    var filename = filenames[i];
    fs.stat(filename, function(err, stats) {
      if (err) throw err;
      if (! stats.isFile()) return readFileAt(i + 1);

      fs.readFile(filename, 'utf8', function(err, text) {
        if (err) throw err;
        concatenation += text;
        if (i + 1 === filenames.length) {
          // all files read, display the output
          return console.log(concatenation);
        }
        readFileAt(i + 1);
      });
    });
  }
  readFileAt(0);
});
```

This is, as you may have noticed, a lot more code than the synchronous version. When we used the synchronous filter and forEach methods, this took about half as many lines and reads much more clearly! Wouldn't it be nice if we could just drop in async equivalents of those wonderful iteration methods? With Async.js, we can do just that!

When It's OK to Throw

You might have noticed that I ignored my own advice from Section 1.4, *Handling Async Errors*, on page 12 in that last code example. Throwing exceptions from callbacks is poor form—in a production environment. However, for a simple example like this, throwing exceptions is perfectly fine. In the unlikely event that this code goes wrong, a throw will shut it down and give us a nice stacktrace explaining why.

The real crime here is that the same error-handling logic, if (err) throw err, is repeated three times! We'll see how Async.js can help us reduce that repetition in *Error Handling in Async.js*, on page 52.

Functional Style with Async.js

We want to replace the filter and forEach methods we used for synchronous iteration with async analogs. Async.js gives us two options.

- async.filter and async.forEach, which process the given array *in parallel*

- async.filterSeries and async.forEachSeries, which process the given array *sequentially*

Running our async operations in parallel would be faster, so why would we want to use a series method? There are two reasons.

- The aforementioned problem of unpredictable ordering. We might get around this by storing our results in an array and then joining it, but that's an extra step.

- There's a limit on the number of files that Node (or any application process) can try to read simultaneously. If we hit that limit, the OS would give us an error. If we read the files sequentially, we don't have to deal with this limitation.

So, we'll stick to async.forEachSeries for now. Here's a straightforward adaptation of our synchronous code to use Async.js's collection methods:

```
Asyncjs/forEachSeries.js
var async = require('async');
var fs = require('fs');
process.chdir('recipes'); // change the working directory
```

```
var concatenation = '';

var dirContents = fs.readdirSync('.');

async.filter(dirContents, isFilename, function(filenames) {
  async.forEachSeries(filenames, readAndConcat, onComplete);
});

function isFilename(filename, callback) {
  fs.stat(filename, function(err, stats) {
    if (err) throw err;
    callback(stats.isFile());
  });
}

function readAndConcat(filename, callback) {
  fs.readFile(filename, 'utf8', function(err, fileContents) {
    if (err) return callback(err);
    concatenation += fileContents;
    callback();
  });
}

function onComplete(err) {
  if (err) throw err;
  console.log(concatenation);
}
```

Now our code splits up nicely into two parts: the overall task (in the form of the async.filter and async.forEachSeries calls) and the implementation details (in the form of two iterator functions and one final callback).

filter and forEach aren't the only Async.js utilities corresponding to standard functional iteration methods. There are also the following:

- reject/rejectSeries, the inverse of filter
- map/mapSeries, for 1:1 transformations
- reduce/reduceRight, for transforming a value at each step
- detect/detectSeries, for finding a value matching a filter
- sortBy, for generating a sorted copy
- some, for testing whether at least one value matches the given criterion
- every, for testing whether *all* values match the given criterion

These methods are the core of Async.js, allowing you to perform common iterations with minimal boilerplate. Before we move on to more advanced methods, let's take a look at the way these methods deal with errors.

Error Handling in Async.js

In our original async code, we had three throws. In the Async.js version, we have two, yet all errors will still be thrown. How does Async.js do it? And why can't we have just one throw?

Simply put, Async.js follows Node conventions. This means that every I/O callback has the form (err, results...)—with the exception of callbacks where the result is a boolean. Boolean callbacks just have the form (result), which is why our isFilename iterator from the previous code example needs to handle errors on its own.

Asyncjs/forEachSeries.js
```
function isFilename(filename, callback) {
  fs.stat(filename, function(err, stats) {
    if (err) throw err;
    callback(stats.isFile());
  });
}
```

Blame Node's fs.exists for setting this precedent. That means that the iterators for the Async.js collection methods (filter, reject, detect, some, every, and their series equivalents) can't report errors.

With all non-boolean Async.js iterators, passing a value other than null or undefined as the first argument to the iterator's callback will immediately invoke the completion callback with that error. That's why readAndConcat can do without throw.

Asyncjs/forEachSeries.js
```
function readAndConcat(filename, callback) {
  fs.readFile(filename, 'utf8', function(err, fileContents) {
    if (err) return callback(err);
    concatenation += fileContents;
    callback();
  });
}
```

So, if callback(err) does get called from readAndConcat, that err will be passed to onComplete. Async.js guarantees that onComplete will be called only once, either the first time an error occurs or after all operations have finished successfully.

Asyncjs/forEachSeries.js
```
function onComplete(err) {
  if (err) throw err;
  console.log(concatenation);
}
```

Node's error conventions may not ideal for Async.js's collection methods. But for all of Async.js's other methods, following these conventions allow errors to flow neatly from individual tasks to the completion callback. We'll see more examples of this in the next section.

4.3 Organizing Tasks with Async.js

Async.js's collection methods solve the problem of applying a single async function to a set of data. But what if, instead of a set of data, we have a set of *functions?* In this section, we'll explore some of the powerful tools that Async.js has for dispatching async functions and collecting their results.

Running an Async Series

Suppose we have an array of async functions that we want to run in order. Without the use of a utility function, we might have to write something like this:

```
funcs[0](function() {
  funcs[1](function() {
    funcs[2](onComplete);
  })
});
```

Fortunately, we have async.series and async.waterfall. Each takes an array of functions (the *task list)* and runs them sequentially, passing each one a Node-style callback. The difference between the two is that async.series provides only the callback to each task, whereas async.waterfall also provides the results from the previous task. (By "results," I mean the nonerror values each task passes to its callback.)

Let's look at a simple demonstration using timeouts.

Asyncjs/seriesTimers.js
```
var async = require ('async');

var start = new Date;

async.series([
  function(callback) { setTimeout(callback, 100); },
  function(callback) { setTimeout(callback, 300); },
  function(callback) { setTimeout(callback, 200); }
], function(err, results) {
  // show time elapsed since start
  console.log('Completed in ' + (new Date - start) + 'ms');
});
```

(Substituting async.waterfall for async.series would have no effect on this example, since each task's callback is run with no arguments.)

The completion handler will run after a little over 600m because each task in the array is completed in order. The callback that Async.js passes to each task function simply asks, "Is there an error (the first argument)? If not, then I'll collect the result (the second argument) and run the next task."

The next time you have a set of async functions that you want to run sequentially, reach for async.series or async.waterfall. There's an excellent chance that one of them is the right tool for the job.

Parallelizing Async Functions

Async.js offers a parallel analog of async.series called async.parallel. Just like async.series, it takes an array of functions of the form function(callback) {...}, plus an (optional) completion handler that runs after the last callback fires.

Let's repeat our timeout example.

```
Asyncjs/parallelTimers.js
var async = require ('async');
var start = new Date;
async.parallel([
  function(callback) { setTimeout(callback, 100); },
  function(callback) { setTimeout(callback, 300); },
  function(callback) { setTimeout(callback, 200); }
], function(err, results) {
  console.log('Completed in ' + (new Date - start) + 'ms');
});
```

Whereas async.series took the sum of the timeouts to complete (~600ms), async.parallel takes only the max timeout (~300ms).

Conveniently, Async.js passes the results to the completion handler in the order corresponding to the task array, not the order in which the results were generated. Thus, you get the performance benefits of parallelism without the unpredictability.

Along with the collection methods, async.series, async.waterfall, and async.parallel are the heart and soul of Async.js: simple, time-saving utility functions for the most common async scenarios.

4.4 Dynamic Async Queuing

Most of the time, the simple methods from the last two sections are enough to solve your async dilemmas. But async.series and async.parallel have their limitations.

- The task array is static. Once you've called async.series or async.parallel, you can't add or remove tasks.

- There's also no way to ask, "How many tasks have been completed?" It's a black box, unless you dispatch updates from the tasks themselves.

- You're limited to either no concurrency or unlimited concurrency. That's a pretty big deal when it comes to file I/O. If we're operating on thousands of files, we don't want to be inefficient by doing a series, but we're likely to anger the OS if we try to do everything in parallel.

Async.js provides a versatile method that addresses every one of these issues: async.queue.

Understanding the Queue

The basic concept underlying async.queue is reminiscent of a DMV; it can handle multiple people simultaneously (up to the number of clerks on duty), but rather than have a separate line for each clerk, it has a single stack of numbers. When you arrive, you get a number. As each clerk becomes free, the clerk calls the next number.

async.queue's interface is a bit more complex than that of async.series and async.parallel. It takes a function called the *worker* (rather than an array of functions) and a *concurrency* value (the maximum number of simultaneous tasks the worker can process). Then it returns a queue that we can push arbitrary task data onto (along with an optional callback).

Here's a trivial example:

```
Asyncjs/simpleQueue.js
var async = require('async');

function worker(data, callback) {
  console.log(data);
  callback();
}
var concurrency = 2;
var queue = async.queue(worker, concurrency);
queue.push(1);
queue.push(2);
queue.push(3);
```

No matter what the concurrency is (as long as it's at least 1), we get the following output:

```
1
2
3
```

There is a difference under the hood, though: with concurrency of 2, we need two trips to the event queue. If it were 1, we'd need three trips, one for each line. And if it were 3 or more, we'd need just one trip.

A queue with concurrency of 0 will do nothing. And if you want maximum concurrency, just use Infinity.

Pushing Tasks

Although queue.push shares the same name as [].push, there are two critical differences.

First,

```
queue.push([1, 2, 3]);
```

is equivalent to the following:

```
queue.push(1);
queue.push(2);
queue.push(3);
```

This means you can't use arrays directly as task data. You can, however, use anything else—even functions. In fact, if you want to use an array of functions like you would with async.series or async.parallel, all you need to do is define a worker that passes its second argument to its first.

```
function worker(task, callback) {
  task(callback);
}
var concurrency = 2;
var queue = async.queue(worker, concurrency);
queue.push(tasks);
```

Second, you can provide a callback function along with each push; if you do, it's given directly to the worker function as the callback argument. So, for instance,

```
queue.push([1, 2, 3], function(err, result) {
  console.log('Task complete!');
});
```

will (assuming that the worker runs its callback) emit the output Task complete! three times. push callbacks are invaluable because async.queue, unlike async.series/async.parallel, doesn't store results internally. If you want them, you'll have to capture them yourself.

Handling Completion

As with async.series and its ilk, we can give async.queue a completion handler. Instead of passing it as an argument, though, we need to attach it as a property called drain. (Picture a tub full of incomplete tasks; when the last one has gone down the drain, the callback fires.) Here's a demonstration with timers:

```
Asyncjs/queueTimers.js
var async = require('async');

function worker(data, callback) {
  setTimeout(callback, data);
}
var concurrency = 2;
var queue = async.queue(worker, concurrency);
var start = new Date;
queue.drain = function() {
  console.log('Completed in ' + (new Date - start) + 'ms');
};

queue.push([100, 300, 200]);
```

Recall that async.series took ~600ms to get through these timeouts (the sum), while async.parallel took only ~300ms (the max). Here, concurrency is 2, so initially, the first two timeouts will run in parallel. But when the 100ms timeout finishes, the next task on the queue (the 200ms timeout) will immediately start. So, in this case, async.queue will finish at about the same time as async.parallel. The order matters: if 300 were the third timeout, the queue would take ~400ms to complete.

Note that we can always push more tasks onto the queue, and drain will fire *every time* the last task on the queue has finished. Unfortunately, this means that async.queue can't give us neatly ordered results the way async.waterfall could. If we want to collect data from our queued tasks, we're on our own.

Advanced Queue Callbacks

Although drain is usually the only handler you'll need, async.queue provides a few other events.

- When the last task has started running, the queue calls empty. (When the task finishes, the queue calls drain.)

- When the concurrency limit is reached, the queue calls saturated.

- If you provide a function as the second argument in a push, it'll be called when the given task (or each task in the given array) is finished.

In this section, we've seen how async.queue is one of the most powerful functions in Async.js. When you need to run a large number of async tasks with limited concurrency, think async.queue.

That's it for our coverage of Async.js, the most widely used and, arguably, most feature-rich JavaScript flow control library. However, I don't want you to get the impression that Async.js is the right tool for every callback-driven job. Let's close out the chapter by looking at one of its top rivals, Step.

4.5 Minimalist Flow Control with Step

Tim Caswell's Step is a lightweight library.[5] In fact, its API consists of a single function: Step.

Step takes a list of functions; here's an example:

```
Step(task1, task2, task3);
```

Each function can control the flow in three ways.

- It can call this to make Step run the next function in the list.
- It can call a callback generated by this.parallel or this.group n times to tell Step to run the next function n times.
- It can return a value, which will also make Step run the next function in the list. This makes it easy to mix synchronous functions with async ones.

The next function will receive the results of its predecessor (that is, its return value or the arguments it passed to this) or the results of all instances of its predecessor if that predecessor was run with this.parallel or this.group. (The difference is that this.parallel provides those results as separate arguments, while this.group merges them into arrays.)

The entire library is, as of this writing, just 152 lines long (with comments) yet is versatile enough to handle most async flows. The downside of this minimalism is that a flow created with Step can be understood only by reading each function in it. Flows created with the everything-but-the-kitchen-sink Async.js tend to be more self-explanatory.

Still, if you feel like rolling up your sleeves, writing Async.js-like utility functions in Step can be a great exercise. For example, here's the equivalent of async.map in just eleven lines:

---

5. https://github.com/creationix/step

Asyncjs/stepMap.js

```
var Step = require('step');

function stepMap(arr, iterator, callback) {
  Step(
    function() {
      var group = this.group();
      for (var i = 0; i < arr.length; i++) {
        iterator(arr[i], group());
      }
    },
    callback
  );
}
```

I find using Step to be a refreshing exercise. While using Async.js is mainly about finding the right utility function for the job, Step encourages you to think problems through clearly and write elegant, efficient solutions.

4.6   What We've Learned

In this chapter, we saw how common async patterns can be implemented with minimal boilerplate using the right flow control functions. Async.js has become the number-one flow control library by offering a robust combination of collection iteration and task-wrangling methods. If you have a flow control problem, the odds are very good that Async.js has a solution. Or if you're more of the do-it-yourself type, consider Step.

Isaac Schlueter, lead developer of the Node.js project, made a very small flow control library called Slide,[6] which is used in npm. In Slide's README, he wrote this:

> You should use it as an example of how to write your own flow control utilities. You'll never fully appreciate a flow control lib that you didn't write yourself.

I hope that's not true. Writing a flow control lib is a good exercise, but you shouldn't have to reinvent the wheel just to see how it works. As the JavaScript ecosystem matures, flow control should become more widespread and more standardized. For the time being, if your application needs flow control, the important thing is to choose a good library and learn it well.

---

6.   https://github.com/isaacs/slide-flow-control

CHAPTER 5

Multithreading with Workers

At the start of this book, I described events as an alternative to multithreading. More precisely, events replace a specific kind of multithreading, the kind where multiple parts of an application process run simultaneously (either virtually, through interrupts, or physically on multiple CPU cores). This gets to be a problem when code running in different threads has access to the same data. Even a line as simple as

```
i++;
```

can be a source of pernicious Heisenbugs[1] when it allows separate threads to modify the same i at the same time. Thankfully, this kind of multithreading is impossible in JavaScript.

On the other hand, distributing tasks across multiple CPU cores is increasingly essential because those cores are no longer making the same exponential gains in efficiency, year after year, that used to be expected. So, we *need* multithreading. Does that mean abandoning event-based programming?

Au contraire! While running on a single thread isn't ideal, naïvely distributing an app across multiple cores can be even worse. Multicore systems slow to a crawl when those cores have to constantly talk to each other to avoid stepping on each other's toes. It's much better to give each core a separate job and then sync up occasionally.

That's precisely what workers do in JavaScript. From the master thread of your application, you tell a worker, "Go run this code in a separate thread." The worker can send you messages (and vice versa), which take the form of (what else?) callbacks run from the event queue. In short, you interact with different threads the same way you do I/O in JavaScript.

---

1.   http://en.wikipedia.org/wiki/Heisenbug

In this chapter, we'll look at workers in both their browser and Node manifestations, and we'll discuss some practical applications.

> ## Threads vs. Processes
>
> In this chapter, I throw around the words *thread* and *process* interchangeably. At the operating system level, there's an important distinction: threads within a process can share state, while separate processes can't. But in JavaScript, concurrent code (as run by workers) never shares state. So, workers may be implemented using lightweight OS threads, but they behave like processes.
>
> There are Node libraries, most notably, Threads-A-GoGo,[a] that allow you to break the state-sharing rule for the sake of efficiency. Those are beyond the scope of this chapter, which is concerned only with concurrency in standard JavaScript.
>
> ---
> a. https://github.com/xk/node-threads-a-gogo

5.1 Web Workers

Web workers are part of the living standard widely known as HTML5. To create one, you call the global Worker constructor with the URL of a script.

```
var worker = new Worker('worker.js');
worker.addEventListener('message', function(e) {
  console.log(e.data);  // echo whatever was sent by postMessage
});
```

(Usually, we want only the data property from the message event. If we were binding the same event handler to multiple workers, we could use e.target to determine which worker emitted the event.)

So, now we know how to listen to workers. Conveniently, the interface for talking to workers is symmetrical: we use worker.postMessage to send it, and the worker uses self.addEventListener('message', ...) to receive it. Here's a complete example:

```
// master script
var worker = new Worker('boknows.js');
worker.addEventListener('message', function(e) {
  console.log(e.data);
});
worker.postMessage('football');
worker.postMessage('baseball');

// boknows.js
self.addEventListener('message', function(e) {
  self.postMessage('Bo knows ' + e.data);
});
```

You can play with the message-passing interface at a little site I created, the Web Worker Sandbox.[2] Any time you create a new example, it gets a unique URL that you can share.

Restrictions on Web Workers

Web workers are primarily intended to handle complex computations without compromising DOM responsiveness. Potential uses include the following:

- Decoding video as it streams in with the Broadway implementation of the H.264 codec[3]

- Encrypting communications with the Stanford JavaScript Crypto Library[4]

- Parsing text in a web-based editor, à la Ace[5]

In fact, Ace already does this by default. When you type code into an Ace-based editor, Ace needs to perform some pretty heavy string analysis before updating the DOM with appropriate syntax highlighting. In modern browsers, that analysis is done on a separate thread, ensuring that the editor remains smooth and responsive.

Typically, the worker will send the result of its computations to the master thread, which will then update the page. Why not update the page directly? Mainly, to keep JavaScript's async abstractions intact. If a worker could alter the page's markup, we'd end up in the same place as Java, wrapping our DOM manipulation code in mutexes and semaphores to avoid race conditions.

Likewise, a worker can't see the global `window` object or any other object in the master thread (or in other worker threads). When an object is sent through `postMessage`, it's transparently serialized and unserialized; think `JSON.parse` `(JSON.stringify(obj))`. So, changes to the original object won't affect the copy in the other thread.

Even the trusty `console` object isn't available to workers. All a worker *can* see is its own global object, called `self`, and everything bundled with it: standard JavaScript objects like `setTimeout` and `Math`, plus the browser's Ajax methods.

Ah yes, Ajax! A worker can use `XMLHttpRequest` freely. It can even use `WebSocket` if the browser supports it. That means the worker can pull data directly from the server. And if we're dealing with a lot of data (like, say, streaming video

---

2. http://webworkersandbox.com/
3. https://github.com/mbebenita/Broadway
4. http://crypto.stanford.edu/sjcl/
5. http://ace.ajax.org/

that needs to be decoded), keeping it in one thread rather than serializing it with postMessage is a big win.

There's also a special importScripts function that will (synchronously) load and run the given script(s).

```
importScripts('https://raw.github.com/gist/1962739/danika.js');
```

Normally, synchronous loading is a big no-no, but remember that we're in a secondary thread here. As long as the worker has nothing else to do, blocking is A-OK.

Which Browsers Support Web Workers?

On the desktop, the Web Worker standard has been implemented in Chrome, Firefox, and Safari for a couple of years, and it's in IE10. Mobile support is spotty as well. The latest iOS Safari supports them, but the latest Android browser doesn't. At the time of this writing, that translates into 59.12 percent browser support, according to Caniuse.com.[6]

In short, you can't count on your site's users having web workers. You can, however, easily write a shim to run the target script normally if window.Worker is unavailable. Web workers are just a performance enhancement after all.

Be careful to test web workers in multiple browsers because there are some critical differences among the implementations. For instance, Firefox allows workers to spawn their own "subworkers," but Chrome currently doesn't.

5.2   Node Workers with cluster

In the early days of Node, there were many competing APIs for multithreading. Most of these solutions were clumsy, requiring users to spin up multiple instances of a server to listen on different TCP ports, which would then be hooked up to the real one via proxy. It was only in the 0.6 release that a standard was included out of the box that allowed multiple processes to bind to the same port: cluster.[7]

Typically, cluster is used to spin up one process per CPU core for optimal performance (though whether each process will actually get its own core is entirely up to the underlying OS).

---

6.   http://caniuse.com/webworkers

7.   http://nodejs.org/docs/latest/api/cluster.html

Multithreading/cluster.js

```
var cluster = require('cluster');
if (cluster.isMaster) {
  // spin up workers
  var coreCount = require('os').cpus().length;
  for (var i = 0; i < coreCount; i++) {
    cluster.fork();
  }
  // bind death event
  cluster.on('death', function(worker) {
    console.log('Worker ' + worker.pid + ' has died');
  });
} else {
  // die immediately
  process.exit();
}
```

The output will look something like

```
Worker 15330 has died
Worker 15332 has died
Worker 15329 has died
Worker 15331 has died
```

with one line for each CPU core.

The code may look baffling at first. The trick is that while web workers load a separate script, cluster.fork() causes the *same* script that it's run from to be loaded in a separate process. The only way the script knows whether it's being run as the master or a worker is by checking cluster.isMaster.

The reason for this design decision is that multithreading in Node has a very different primary use case than multithreading in the browser. While the browser can relegate any surplus threads to background tasks, Node servers need to scale up the computational resources available for their main task: handling requests.

(External scripts can be run as separate processes using child_process.fork.[8] Its capabilities are largely identical to those of cluster.fork—in fact, cluster uses child_process under the hood—except that child process can't share TCP ports.)

Talking to Node Workers

As with web workers, cluster workers can communicate with the master process by sending message events, and vice versa. The API is slightly different, though.

---

8.   http://nodejs.org/docs/latest/api/child_process.html

Multithreading/clusterMessage.js

```
var cluster = require('cluster');
if (cluster.isMaster) {
  // spin up workers
  var coreCount = require('os').cpus().length;
  for (var i = 0; i < coreCount; i++) {
    var worker = cluster.fork();
    worker.send('Hello, Worker!');
    worker.on('message', function(message) {
      if (message._queryId) return;
      console.log(message);
    });
  }
} else {
  process.send('Hello, main process!');
  process.on('message', function(message) {
    console.log(message);
  });
}
```

The output will look something like

```
Hello, main process!
Hello, main process!
Hello, Worker!
Hello, Worker!
Hello, main process!
Hello, Worker!
Hello, main process!
Hello, Worker!
```

where the order is unpredictable, because each thread is racing to console.log first. (You'll have to manually terminate the process with Ctrl+C.)

As with web workers, the API is symmetric, with a send call on one side triggering a 'message' event on the other side. But notice that the argument to send (or rather, a serialized copy) is given directly by the 'message' event, rather than being attached as the data property.

Notice the line

```
if (message._queryId) return;
```

in the master message handler? Node sometimes sends its own messages from the workers, which always look something like this:

```
{ cmd: 'online', _queryId: 1, _workerId: 1 }
```

It's safe to ignore these internal messages, but be aware that they're used to perform some important magic behind the scenes. Most notably, when workers try to listen on a TCP port, Node uses internal messages to allow the port to be shared.

Restrictions on Node Workers

For the most part, cluster obeys the same rules as web workers: there's a master, and there are workers; they communicate via events with attached strings or serializable objects. However, while workers are obviously second-class citizens in the browser, Node's workers possess all the rights and privileges of the master except, notably, the following:

- The ability to shut down the application
- The ability to spawn more workers
- The ability to communicate with each other

This gives the master the burden of being a hub for all interthread communication. Fortunately, this inconvenience can be abstracted away with a library like Roly Fentanes' Clusterhub.[9]

In this section, we've seen how workers have become an integral part of Node, allowing a server to utilize multiple cores without running multiple application instances. Node's cluster API allows the same script to run concurrently, with one master process and any number of workers. To minimize the overhead of communication, shared state should be stored in an external database, such as Redis.

5.3 What We've Learned

It's early, but I'd say the future of multicore JavaScript is bright. For any application that can be split up into largely independent processes that need to talk to each other only periodically, workers are a winning solution for leveraging maximum CPU power. Distributed computing has never been more fun.

---

9. https://github.com/fent/clusterhub

CHAPTER 6

Async Script Loading

In the beginning, there was this:

```
<script src="allMyClientSideCode.js"></script>
```

And it was…not great. "Where should it go?" developers wondered. "Up in the
<head>? Or down in the <body>?" For script-heavy sites, both options lead to
misery. A large script in the <head> delays all page rendering, giving the user
a "White Screen of Death"[1] until the script loads completely. But a large script
at the end of the <body> gives the user a lifeless, static page littered with
nonworking controls and empty boxes where client-side rendering is supposed
to occur.

The ideal solution to this problem is to triage your scripts; those that are
needed for the page to look and feel right should load right away. Scripts that
can wait should. But what's the right way of delaying those scripts while
ensuring that they're available when called?

In the last few years, several technologies aimed at solving this problem have
become widespread. In this chapter, we'll look at how HTML5's async and defer
attributes can help. We'll also look at two popular script-loading libraries:
yepnope and Require.js.

Async Loading in Node.js

We'll be sticking to the browser in this chapter, because async module loading in
Node is rarely useful. Node once offered an async variant of require, but it was removed
in version 0.3. If you're interested in the reasoning behind its removal, see
https://groups.google.com/d/msg/nodejs/y_-LZqltb1A/mmpYLlLurqkJ.

---

1. The term was coined by the authors of the excellent *JavaScript Performance Rocks*:
http://javascriptrocks.com/performance/.

6.1 Limitations and Caveats

Before we continue, here are a few important things to note:

- The techniques in this chapter are not compatible with scripts that are inlined (defined directly in your page's markup). Inlining should be avoided when possible. If you must inline a script, don't try to use the defer or async attribute on it.

- When using any of the techniques in this chapter, you should not use document.write. Its behavior in asynchronously loaded scripts is unpredictable. If you don't know what document.write is, then good. Suffice to say it's the GOTO of DOM manipulation.

- This is not a definitive guide. I've neglected some important platform-specific details for the sake of brevity. For example, certain mobile browsers will refuse to cache scripts larger than a certain size. So, if you're targeting those devices, it's important to keep scripts small.

Page load optimization is a rich subject on which whole books have been written, and script loading is just one factor. But for script-heavy sites that aren't taking advantage of async loading, there's plenty of low-hanging fruit to be picked using the techniques in this chapter.

6.2 Reintroducing the <script> Tag

At the risk of sounding hyperbolic, <script> is the most important HTML tag of all time. Don't believe me? Consider that a page consisting entirely of a single script tag can do anything. It can spin itself a document from whole cloth, loading whatever resources it wants. By contrast, even the most marvelous page without a <script> tag is sharply limited, unable to respond to the user's actions with anything more complicated than a CSS transition.

In modern browsers, <script> comes in two refreshing flavors: classic and nonblocking. In this section, we'll see how you can use both varieties to make your pages load as quickly as possible.

Where the Blocking Scripts Go

A standard-issue <script> tag is commonly said to be *blocking*. That term has to be understood in context: when a modern browser sees a blocking <script> tag, it will continue to read the document past that point and download other resources (scripts and style sheets). However, it won't evaluate those resources until the script has been fully downloaded and run.

So, if you have five blocking <script> tags in the <head> of the document, the user won't see anything but the page's title until all five scripts have been downloaded and run. Further, while those scripts are being run, they'll be able to see the document only up until that point. If they want to see any of the good stuff that's waiting down in the <body>, they'll have to bind a handler to an event like document.onreadystatechange.

For that reason, it's become fashionable to put scripts at the end of the page's <body>. This way, the user gets to see the page more quickly, and the scripts get to see the DOM in all its glory without having to wait for an event to fire. For most scripts, this move is a big improvement.

But not all scripts are alike. Before you move a script down, ask yourself three questions.

- Is there a chance that this script will be called directly from inlined JavaScript in the <body>? This may be obvious, but it's worth double-checking.
- Does this script allow older browsers to recognize HTML5 elements? Modernizr[2] does, which is why the HTML5 Boilerplate[3]—an exemplar of best practices—includes it right up top.
- Is this script something that will determine how your page looks when it's rendered? An example is Typekit's hosted fonts. If you put Typekit's script at the end of your document, the text on your page will render twice: once immediately and again after the script runs.

If the answer is "yes" to any of these questions, that script should go in the <head>. Otherwise, it should go in the <body>. Minifying and concatenating those two sets of scripts will give you a document that looks like this:

```
<html>
<head>
  <!-- metadata and stylesheets go here -->
  <script src="headScripts.js"></scripts>
</head>
<body>
  <!-- content goes here -->
  <script src="bodyScripts.js"></script>
</body>
</html>
```

This is great for load times, but be aware that it may give the user a chance to interact with the page before bodyScripts.js is loaded.

---

2. http://modernizr.com/
3. http://html5boilerplate.com/

Deferring Scripts

In the last section, I recommended <body> placement for most scripts, since that allows the user to see the page more quickly and avoids the overhead of binding to a "ready" event before manipulating the DOM. But there is a downside: the browser won't be able to start loading those scripts until the whole document is loaded. For large documents being sent over slow connections, this can be a major bottleneck.

Ideally, we'd load those scripts in parallel with the document, without delaying DOM rendering. Then when the document is ready, we'd run the scripts because they're loaded while preserving the order of the <script> tags.

If you've read the book up to this point, no doubt you're excited about writing a custom Ajax script loader to meet these requirements! But most browsers support a simpler solution.

```
<script defer src="deferredScript.js">
```

Adding that defer attribute tells the browser this: "Start loading this script right away, but don't run it until the document is ready and all previous scripts with defer have finished running." Placing a deferred script in the <head> of your document gives you all the advantages of <body> placement, plus a substantial speed boost in large documents!

The downside? defer isn't supported by all browsers. Notably, as of this writing, even the latest Opera ignores the attribute.[4] That means if you want to ensure that your deferred scripts run after the document is loaded, you'll have to wrap each script's code in something like jQuery's $(document).ready. That may be worthwhile, since something like 97 percent of your visitors will get to enjoy the benefits of parallel loading, while the other 3 percent will still get perfectly functional JavaScript.

With defer, we can improve on the page example from the previous section by replacing bodyScripts.js with deferredScripts.js.

```
<html>
<head>
  <!-- metadata and stylesheets go here -->
  <script src="headScripts.js"></scripts>
  <script defer src="deferredScripts.js"></script>
</head>
<body>
  <!-- content goes here -->
</body>
</html>
```

---

4.   http://caniuse.com/#search=defer

Just remember that it's important to wrap deferredScripts so that it won't run until after the document ready event in browsers that don't support defer. If the body content is more than a couple of kilobytes, that trade-off is worthwhile.

Full Script Parallelization

If you're a hardcore every-millisecond-counts page load gearhead, defer may sound like weak sauce to you. You don't want to wait until all previous scripts with defer have run. And you certainly don't want those scripts to wait to run until the document is ready, not when they have to use $(document).ready anyway for Opera's sake. You just want to load those scripts *as soon as possible* and run them *as soon as possible*.

That's why modern browsers offer the async attribute.

```
<script async src="speedyGonzales.js">
<script async src="roadRunner.js">
```

If defer makes you think of an orderly queue waiting for the document to load, async should make you think of anarchy. Those two scripts shown earlier could run in any order, and they'll run as soon as the JavaScript engine is available to run them, whether the document is ready or not. So, aside from feeling the need for speed, why would you use async?

For most scripts, async is a tough sell. It's not as widely supported as defer, so fewer users will notice the performance boost.[5] And because async scripts can run at any time, it's all too easy to introduce Heisenbugs that depend on when a script happens to finish loading.

But for scripts that are intended to be independent, async is a small but significant win. Got a third-party script that adds a feedback widget and another that adds a tech support chat box? The page will run fine without them, and it doesn't matter which one runs first. So, you can get a free speed boost by using async with them.

Async + Defer = ?

You might be asking, "What if I use both defer and async on the same script?" The answer is that async overrides defer in browsers that support both. Since defer is more widely supported and provides the main benefit of async—allowing the DOM to render while the script downloads—I recommend using defer whenever you use async.

---

5.   http://caniuse.com/#search=async

Adding a couple of independent widgets to our last page example, we get the following:

```html
<html>
<head>
  <!-- metadata and stylesheets go here -->
  <script src="headScripts.js"></scripts>
  <script src="deferredScripts.js" defer></script>
</head>
<body>
  <!-- content goes here -->
  <script async defer src="feedbackWidget.js"></script>
  <script async defer src="chatWidget.js"></script>
</body>
</html>
```

This page structure makes your priorities clear. In the vast majority of browsers, DOM rendering will be delayed only until headScripts.js finishes running. deferredScripts.js will load in the background while the DOM is rendered. Then, after DOM rendering, deferredScripts.js and the two widget scripts will run. The order in which those scripts run is indeterminate in browsers that support async. If you're not sure whether that's OK, don't use async!

In this section, we've seen how a <script> tag's placement and attributes you use can make a big difference in the time it takes for someone to start using your page. In the next section, we'll see how you can take the principle of async loading even further by using scripts to load other scripts.

6.3 Programmatic Loading

While <script> tags are appealingly simple, there are some situations that require a more sophisticated approach to script loading. Perhaps we want a certain script to load only for users who meet certain requirements, such as premium subscribers or gamers who've reached a certain level. Or we may want a certain feature, like a chat widget, to load only when the user clicks to activate it.

In this section, we'll look at how scripts can load other scripts. After a brief look at low-level approaches, we'll look at two popular libraries that make script loading a breeze: yepnope and Require.js.

Loading Scripts Directly

At the browser API level, there are two (reasonable) ways to fetch a script from a server and run it.

- Make an Ajax request and then eval the response.
- Insert a <script> tag into the DOM.

The latter approach is nicer, since the browser takes care of the work of making an HTTP request for you. Plus, eval has practical problems: leaking scope, making a mess of debugging, and possibly degrading performance. So, to load a script called feature.js, we would insert a <script> tag with some code like this:

```
var head = document.getElementsByTagName('head')[0];
var script = document.createElement('script');
script.src = '/js/feature.js';
head.appendChild(script);
```

But wait—how do we find out when the script has finished loading? We could, of course, add some code in the script itself to trigger an event, but adding that code to every script we load would be a chore (or, in the case of scripts on a third-party server, impossible). The HTML5 specification defines an onload attribute that we can bind a callback to.

```
script.onload = function() {
  // now we can call functions defined in script
};
```

However, onload isn't supported in IE8 and older, which instead uses onreadys-tatechange. There are also some weird edge cases in certain browsers when inserting <script> tags. And I haven't even gotten into error handling! To avoid all of these headaches, I highly recommend using a script-loading library.

Conditional Loading with yepnope

yepnope[6] is a simple and lightweight library (just 1.7KB minified and gzipped) designed to serve the most common dynamic loading needs without frills. It can be used on its own or as part of the Modernizr feature detection library.

At its simplest, yepnope loads a script and gives you a callback for when the script has run.

```
yepnope({
  load: 'oompaLoompas.js',
  callback: function() {
    console.log('Oompa-Loompas ready!');
  }
});
```

---

6.   http://yepnopejs.com/

Not impressed yet? Let's use yepnope to load multiple scripts in parallel and run them in the given order. For example, suppose we want to load Backbone.js, which depends on Underscore.js. All we have to do is provide the two script locations in an array as the load parameter.

```
yepnope({
  load: ['underscore.js', 'backbone.js'],
  complete: function() {
    // Backbone logic goes here
  }
});
```

Notice that we used complete instead of callback here. The difference is that callback is run for every resource in the load list, while complete runs only after everything has been loaded.

yepnope's trademark feature is *conditional loading*. Given a test parameter, yepnope can load different resources based on whether that value is truthy. For instance, if you're using Modernizr, you can determine (to some degree of accuracy) whether the user is on a touchscreen device and load different stylesheets and scripts accordingly.

```
yepnope({
  test: Modernizr.touch,
  yep: ['touchStyles.css', 'touchApplication.js'],
  nope: ['mouseStyles.css', 'mouseApplication.js'],
  complete: function() {
    // either way, the application is now ready!
  }
});
```

With a handful of lines of code, we've set the stage to give users a completely different experience based on their input device. Of course, we don't need both a yep and a nope for every condition. One of the most common uses of yepnope is loading shims to fill in functionality that's missing from older browsers.

```
yepnope({
  test: window.json,
  nope: ['json2.js'],
  complete: function() {
    // now we can JSON safely
  }
});
```

Here's a good markup structure for a page that uses yepnope:

```
<html>
<head>
  <!-- metadata and stylesheets go here -->
  <script src="headScripts.js"></scripts>
  <script src="deferredScripts.js" defer></script>
</head>
<body>
  <!-- content goes here -->
</body>
</html>
```

Look familiar? This is the same structure we had in the section on defer. The only difference is that yepnope.js has been concatenated into one of the script files (likely at the top of deferredScripts.js), and anything that we need conditionally (because the browser needs a shim) or want to load dynamically (in response to a user action) can be loaded separately. The result should be a smaller deferredScripts.js.

I love yepnope. For relatively simple applications that just want to grab a few shims or load a feature when a user clicks something, yepnope is pretty much perfect. For truly voluminous applications, though, something stronger is called for.

Smart Loading with Require.js and AMD

Require.js is the script loader of choice for developers who want to turn the chaos of script-heavy applications into something more orderly. It's a powerful package capable of sorting out even the most complex dependency graphs automatically with AMD.

We'll get to AMD in a moment, but first let's look at a simple script-loading example with Require.js's eponymous function.

```
require(['moment'], function(moment) {
  console.log(moment().format('dddd'));  // day of the week
});
```

The require function takes an array of script names and loads all of those scripts in parallel. Unlike yepnope, Require.js doesn't ensure that the target scripts run in order. Instead, it ensures that they run in an order such that each script's dependencies are satisfied, provided that those scripts are specified via the *Asynchronous Module Definition* (AMD).

AMD is a specification[7] that aims to do for the browser what the CommonJS standard has accomplished for the server. (Node.js modules are based on the

---

7.   https://github.com/amdjs/amdjs-api/wiki/AMD

CommonJS standard.) It mandates a global function (provided by Require.js) called define, which takes three parameters: a name, a list of dependencies, and a callback for when those dependencies are loaded. For example, this is a valid AMD definition for an application that depends on jQuery:

```
define('myApplication' ['jquery'], function($) {
  $('<body>').append('<p>Hello, async world!</p>');
});
```

Notice that the jQuery object, $, is passed to the callback. In fact, the callback will always receive an argument corresponding to each item in the dependency list. You might be wondering how define knew to capture the jQuery object. The answer is that jQuery's own AMD definition[8] returns jQuery from its define callback, thereby declaring "this is my exported object."

```
define( "jquery", [], function () { return jQuery; } );
```

There's a little more to AMD than that, but that's the essence. Adding AMD definitions to every script in your application means you can call require and rest assured that your callback won't be invoked until not only are your direct dependencies met but their dependencies and their dependencies' dependencies are as well, all loading with maximum parallelism and running in an order consistent with the dependency graph.

Sounds great, right? But there's a flip side: while AMD has gotten some traction in the JavaScript community, there are plenty of doubters. Jeremy Ashkenas, for instance, has declined to add the requisite boilerplate to his popular Underscore.js and Backbone.js libraries, awaiting an anticipated ECMAScript module standard. As a result, you can't count on third-party modules to have their own AMD definitions. Choosing AMD can make your application more consistent, but it can also be a recipe for boilerplate code.

In these last few pages, we've seen how you can load a script at runtime via DOM manipulation, and we've looked at two libraries for simplifying that process: yepnope, a small, precise tool, and Require.js, a large and powerful one. Which you choose ultimately depends on what kind of application you're developing and what kind of development team you are. The more "enterprise-y" the application and the bigger the front-end team, the more likely you are to benefit from the AMD-style modularization encouraged by Require.js.

---

8.   See https://github.com/jquery/jquery/blob/master/src/exports.js#L17.

6.4   What We've Learned

You can make your site much snappier by asynchronously loading the scripts you don't need right away. The easiest way to do that is with judicious use of the `defer` and `async` attributes. If you need to load scripts conditionally, consider a loader like yepnope. And if your site has scores of interdependent scripts, take a good look at Require.js. Choose the right tool for the job, embrace it, and enjoy.

And on that note, we've reached the end of the book. Thanks for taking the time to read it. It was my pleasure to write it. No matter where your JavaScript journey takes you from here, I hope that it's rich in beautiful, event-driven code.

Tools for Taming JavaScript

This appendix is an overview of some of the more popular tools for writing async JavaScript code in a more synchronous style. None of these tools is a substitute for a proper understanding of JavaScript events. Instead, they can complement that understanding by adding a few more tricks to your async repertoire.

A1.1 TameJS

The OkCupid team has created a clever precompiler with more than 600 GitHub watchers (http://tamejs.org/) that adds two keywords to JavaScript, await and defer. An await block defines code that won't return until each async task defined with defer has been completed.

```
await {
  setTimeout(defer(), 100);
}
console.log("this will run after the 100ms timeout");
```

The TameJS folks have also created a CoffeeScript fork with the same await/defer mechanism called IcedCoffeeScript ((http://maxtaco.github.com/coffee-script/).

A1.2 StratifiedJS

StratifiedJS (http://onilabs.com/stratifiedjs) is an alternative to the await/defer paradigm that offers finer-grained control structures, with intuitive names like waitfor and resume.

```
console.log('this code will run right away...');
waitfor() {
  setTimeout(resume, 500);
}
console.log('...and this will run 500ms later.');
```

Although not widely used, StratifiedJS is an ambitious project that's received praise from the likes of John Resig (the creator of jQuery).[1] Note that StratifiedJS is the name of the specification, not the implementation; the official reference implementation is called Oni Apollo.[2]

A1.3 Kaffeine

Kaffeine is a precompiler that touts itself as "Extended JavaScript."[3] Among other features, the language offers a simple syntactic sugar for un-nesting callbacks: just add ! after an async function's name. Kaffeine assumes that the function takes a callback as its last argument and simply transforms all code after that call into the callback.

For example, in a jQuery application, it's common to want everything to run from within a $ callback (after the document is ready). With Kaffeine, that's easily done.

```
$!()
alert('The document is ready.');
```

Although it doesn't have as big a following as CoffeeScript, features like this make Kaffeine well worth checking out. The CoffeeScript forks Coco and LiveScript have a similar feature, which it calls *backcalls*. In Coco/LiveScript, the previous example would be written like this:

```
<- $
alert 'The document is ready'
```

The Kaffeine/Coco/LiveScript approach provides much of the power of TameJS/StratifiedJS, with less of a learning curve.

A1.4 Streamline.js

Like Kaffeine, Streamline.js[4] provides a special syntax for transforming the code after an async function call into its callback. Just use _ in place of the callback argument.

```
for (var s = 1; s < 60; s++) {
  setTimeout(_, 1000);
  console.log(s + ' seconds have elapsed');
}
console.log('1 minute has elapsed');
```

---

1. https://twitter.com/jeresig/statuses/164496725254479872
2. https://github.com/onilabs/apollo
3. http://weepy.github.com/kaffeine/index.html
4. https://github.com/Sage/streamlinejs

Interestingly, Streamline can generate either standard callback-driven Java-Script or fiber-based code for node-fibers (see the next section). Also, unlike most other JavaScript precompilers, Streamline can be used in conjunction with CoffeeScript.

Note that Streamline expects callbacks to follow the Node-style argument list convention (err, results...), which eases error handling in Node but makes it difficult to use for browser development.

A1.5 Node-Fibers

While the other projects I've listed here merely compile to plain JavaScript, node-fibers actually extends the language understood by the Node runtime by adding threadlike constructs called *fibers* (http://en.wikipedia.org/wiki/Fiber_(computer_science)). A fiber can yield to other fibers, suspending its own execution until an event causes it run again.

```
var fiber = Fiber.current;
console.log('Yielding until the timeout elapses...')
setTimeout(function() {
  fiber.run();
}, 1000);
Fiber.yield();
console.log('...1 second later');
```

The main advantage of node-fibers over JavaScript precompilers is debugging. The line numbers in node-fiber stack traces correspond to the line numbers in node-fiber source code, and thrown exceptions can be caught even when a fiber yields within a try/catch block.

A1.6 The Future of JavaScript: Generators

The latest iteration of ECMAScript (the specification that all mainstream JavaScript runtimes implement) defines a new JavaScript feature called *generators*. A generator is a special type of function containing a yield statement. A yield is like a return, except that the generator resumes from that yield statement the next time it's run.

Conceptually, generators are a little tricky. However, Mozilla's Task.js (http://taskjs.org/) library shows how they can make async code simpler. Because generators can be resumed, you can write code like this:

```
task.spawn(function() {
  console.log("Yielding...");
  yield task.sleep(1000);
  console.log("...resuming 1 second later");
});
```

Here's how this code works: task.spawn runs our generator, which is just a normal function except for the yield. task.sleep returns a Promise (see Chapter 3, *Promises and Deferreds*, on page 31) that resolves in 1000ms. task.spawn takes that Promise and attaches our generator as its resolve callback. When the Promise resolves, our generator is called again, resuming after the yield. It may sound complicated, but it works beautifully.

ECMAScript 6 (aka Harmony) hasn't been finalized yet. Currently, the only major implementation of generators is in the Firefox browser, and they're enabled only if you specify a JavaScript version of at least 1.7 in your <script> tags, like so:

```
<script type="application/javascript;version=1.7">
```

If generators appeal to you, there is a tool that allows you to compile code that uses generators (and other ECMAScript 5+ features) into widely supported JavaScript code: Google's Traceur.[5]

---

5.   http://code.google.com/p/traceur-compiler/

The Pragmatic Bookshelf

The Pragmatic Bookshelf features books written by developers for developers. The titles continue the well-known Pragmatic Programmer style and continue to garner awards and rave reviews. As development gets more and more difficult, the Pragmatic Programmers will be there with more titles and products to help you stay on top of your game.

Visit Us Online

This Book's Home Page
http://pragprog.com/titles/tbajs
Source code from this book, errata, and other resources. Come give us feedback, too!

Register for Updates
http://pragprog.com/updates
Be notified when updates and new books become available.

Join the Community
http://pragprog.com/community
Read our weblogs, join our online discussions, participate in our mailing list, interact with our wiki, and benefit from the experience of other Pragmatic Programmers.

New and Noteworthy
http://pragprog.com/news
Check out the latest pragmatic developments, new titles and other offerings.

Save on the eBook

Save on the eBook versions of this title. Owning the paper version of this book entitles you to purchase the electronic versions at a terrific discount.

PDFs are great for carrying around on your laptop—they are hyperlinked, have color, and are fully searchable. Most titles are also available for the iPhone and iPod touch, Amazon Kindle, and other popular e-book readers.

Buy now at *http://pragprog.com/coupon*

Contact Us

Online Orders:	*http://pragprog.com/catalog*
Customer Service:	*support@pragprog.com*
International Rights:	*translations@pragprog.com*
Academic Use:	*academic@pragprog.com*
Write for Us:	*http://pragprog.com/write-for-us*
Or Call:	+1 800-699-7764

CPSIA information can be obtained at www.ICGtesting.com
Printed in the USA
LVOW03s0134270314

379052LV00019B/137/P